MORBIER CLOCKS

History, Identification, and Repair

Lawrence A. Seymour

Library of Congress Cataloging-in-Publication Data

Seymour, Lawrence A.
   Morbier clocks: history, identification, and repair / Lawrence A. Seymour.
      p. cm.
   Includes bibliographical references.
   ISBN 978-0-9823584-0-5
   1. Clocks and watches--France--Morbier--History. I. Title.
NK7495.F7S49 2009
681.1'13094447--dc22
                                2009012964

© 2009 by National Association of Watch and Clock Collectors, Inc.
17 16 15 14 13   2 3 4 5

All rights reserved. No part of this publication may be stored in a
retrieval system, reproduced, or transmitted in any form by any means,
electronic, mechanical, photocopying, recording, or otherwise,
without written permission from the publisher.

Printed in the United States of America
The National Association of Watch and Clock Collectors, Inc.
Editor: Diana M. De Lucca; Associate Editor: Freda Conner; Associate Editor: Amy L. Klinedinst
Editor for this project: Bob Reichel, *FNAWCC 28538, January 2008.

Requests to use material from this work should be directed to:
The National Association of Watch and Clock Collectors, Inc.
514 Poplar Street, Columbia, PA 17512

Founded in 1943, the National Association of Watch and Clock Collectors, Inc. (NAWCC) is a nonprofit
20,000-plus member organization whose purpose is to encourage and stimulate interest in the art
and science of horology for the benefit of NAWCC members and the public.
For more information about the NAWCC and an application form please see the back page of this book.

All images in this publication are courtesy of the NAWCC unless otherwise noted.

This book is made up of a four-part series of articles written by Lawrence A. Seymour
and first published in the NAWCC BULLETIN, as follows:
April 1972 (Vol. XV, No. 3, Whole number 157)
February 1973 (Vol. XV, No. 8, Whole number 162)
October 1974 (Vol. XVI, No. 6, Whole number 172)
June 1977 (Vol. XIX, No. 3, Whole number 188)

Since this material was originally published, additional historical and technical information has been reported to the NAWCC BULLETIN and the Library and Research Center, some of which is included in the Bibliography in this book. For additional information refer to the NAWCC BULLETIN Index and submit research requests to the NAWCC Library and Research Center. See: www.nawcc.org

The front cover features a later brass-front clock with a religious-nautical motif.
A young man is receiving a cross as he is about to set out to sea (see page 11).
The back cover features the front view of a three-train, three-bell clock (see page 43).

Table of Contents

Introduction and Historical Notes 1

WHAT IS A MORBIER? 1
Where Do They Come From? 3
How Did They Get Started? 4
How Old Are They? 4
The Early Morbier 4
The Bronze-Front Morbier 6
The Brass-Front Morbier 9
The Later Brass Front 11
Decline of the Morbier 12
Cases for Morbier Movements 14

THE TIME TRAIN 16
The Verge Escapement 16
The Time Train 19
Earlier Verge Movements 20
The Anchor Escapement 22
The Pinwheel Escapement 24

STRIKING TRAINS 27
The Basic Mechanism 27
The Gong Strike 32
The Morez Striking Mechanism 33
Quarter Strike Mechanisms 34
Two-Train, Three-Bell Quarter Strike 35
Three-Train, Three-Bell Striking Mechanisms 37
How to Live with a Morbier 39
Alarm Mechanism 40
Calendar Mechanism 41
Historical Notes 42

RESTORATION AND REPAIR 45
Disassembly 46
Cleaning 57
Checking and Restoring before Assembly 58
Reassembly and Checking the Time Train 58
Motion Work 61
Assembling and Checking the Strike Train 62
Final Assembly 64
Under Dial Work 64

Bibliography 66

About the Author

Lawrence Alan Seymour (1915-2007) was a member of NAWCC since the early 1960s and received the Star Fellow award, the highest member honor. His higher education came from Kenyon College, where he was Phi Beta Kappa in European History and Technology. During World War II he was an officer in naval intelligence. Following the war he was with the U.S. government in numerous state department postings, and during his work with UNESCO in Paris, he pursued his lifelong fascination with timekeeping, salvaging an extensive collection of Morbier clocks from Parisian flea markets. Alan was awarded NAWCC Fellow and Star Fellow. He regularly helped the NAWCC BULLETIN Answer Box with expert knowledge on French clocks. His NAWCC chapter affiliations included Chapters 50, 78, and 135 where he presented numerous programs on Morbier and other French clocks.

Acknowledgments

The foregoing is based on personal experience in restoring Morbier clocks over a period of years. In the original published articles, the author thanked Jean Moreau, director of the Ecole d'Horlogerie d'Anet, and many other friends, amateur and professional, French and American, for their advice and assistance. Without their help and encouragement this treatise could not have been written.

The following individuals provided permission to use photographs of their clocks for this treatise: Wm. G. Foulkes, of Brussels, for permission to use photographs of his clock in Figures 7, 8, and 9. Col. Lynn Moore, Fairfax, VA, for Figures 5, 6, and 10. Renaud Inelan, 78 Le Perray-en-Yvelines, France, for Figures 7 and 16. Other clocks shown were in the author's collection and photos were made by the author.

The Impetus Behind This Reprint

In an email dated May 14, 2005, to NAWCC Editor Diana DeLucca, Lawrence Alan Seymour wrote, "Some years ago I wrote a series of articles for the NAWCC BULLETIN on the subject of Morbier clocks. Since that time very little on Morbier clocks has appeared in the BULLETIN. There are hundreds of these unusual French clocks in the hands of NAWCC members who, I am sure, would be glad to learn more about them. I would like to suggest that one of your editorial assistants review these articles and perhaps combine them into a single article for publication in the BULLETIN or as a reprint. The most useful part is that on the restoration and repair because the Morbier movement is quite different from most other French, English, American and German clocks.

"Please let me know if I can be of assistance in this matter."

Lawrence Seymour did provide assistance. He sent all of the photos he had from the original articles to the NAWCC Publications Department. An editorial assistant did review the published articles, but the project languished until Bob Riechel agreed to help edit the new digital files. This new and improved version of Lawrence Seymour's excellent articles, which includes larger and higher quality images wherever possible, is available for a new generatons of collectors because of the generous assistance of Bob Reichel.

MORBIER CLOCKS

Introduction and Historical Notes

When most Americans think of French clocks, they usually have a childhood memory of seeing a vintage 1900 mantel clock in black marble or a crystal regulator with mercury pendulum and the name Tiffany or Wanamaker on the dial. These clocks, together with the four-column Empire style, were imported in considerable numbers during the late nineteenth and early twentieth centuries and were a favorite wedding present for those who could afford them. For the serious clock collector there has been a tremendous variety of French clocks from which to choose, reflecting the finest workmanship and going back to the early seventeenth century. These were one-of-a-kind masterpieces in which the case was at least as important, if not more so, than the movement and were built for royalty, the nobility, or the wealthy bourgeoisie. Most of these that date from the eighteenth century are now priced out of reach for all but the most affluent, and even the reproductions made in the same styles during the late nineteenth century bring substantial prices.

It is only recently that Americans have become aware that, during the same period that these clocks for the aristocracy were being made in Paris and other major cities, a homely clock "of the people, by the people, and for the people" was being made in substantial numbers in the then remote mountain provinces of the Jura (see Figure 3), a mountain range in eastern France and western Switzerland. Annual production of these so-called Morbier clocks reached about 80,000 from 1860 to 1880 and then tapered off, ending finally during World War I. While this number is small compared to the production of even a single factory in Connecticut during the same period, it is a considerable achievement when one looks at the product and understands the methods of production.

What Is a Morbier?

Figure 1 shows the typical Morbier clock of the late nineteenth century exhibiting these external characteristics: enameled dial bearing the name of the clock merchant (not the maker) and his city, stamped brass hands and the fronton[2] or dial embellishment of thin repousse or embossed brass, depicting a romantic scene, usually with a rural background. Associated with such a clock was a pendulum, also of repousse brass with fanciful decoration of flowers, fruit and even animated figures (see Figure 11), and frequently painted in simple bright colors.

Figure 1. The classic Morbier, made in quantity from 1860 to 1915.

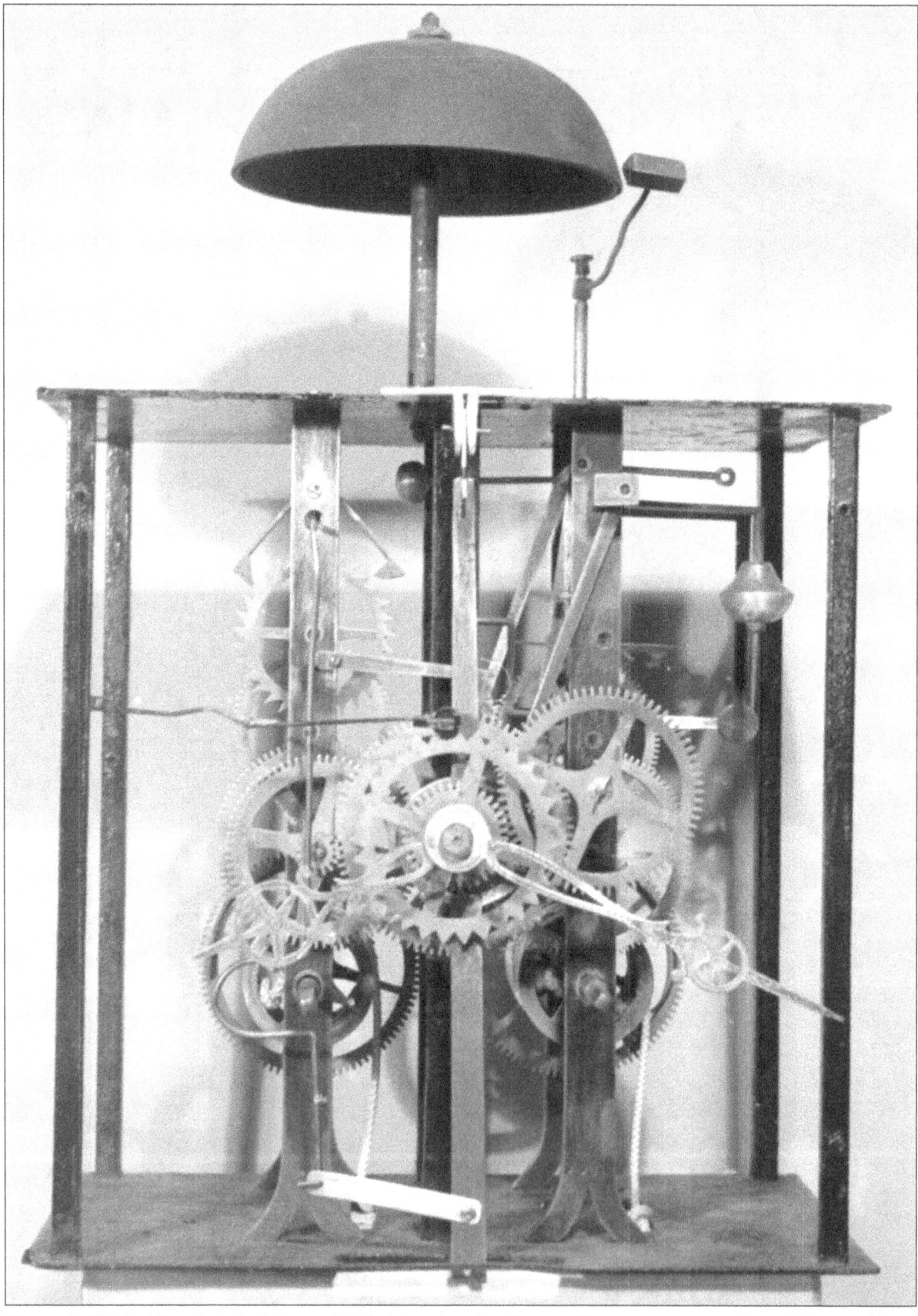

Figure 2. Behind the dial of a late model Morbier, showing the recoil escapement, and pendulum rod in front, with slotted brass suspension spring. This model also has a calendar mechanism.

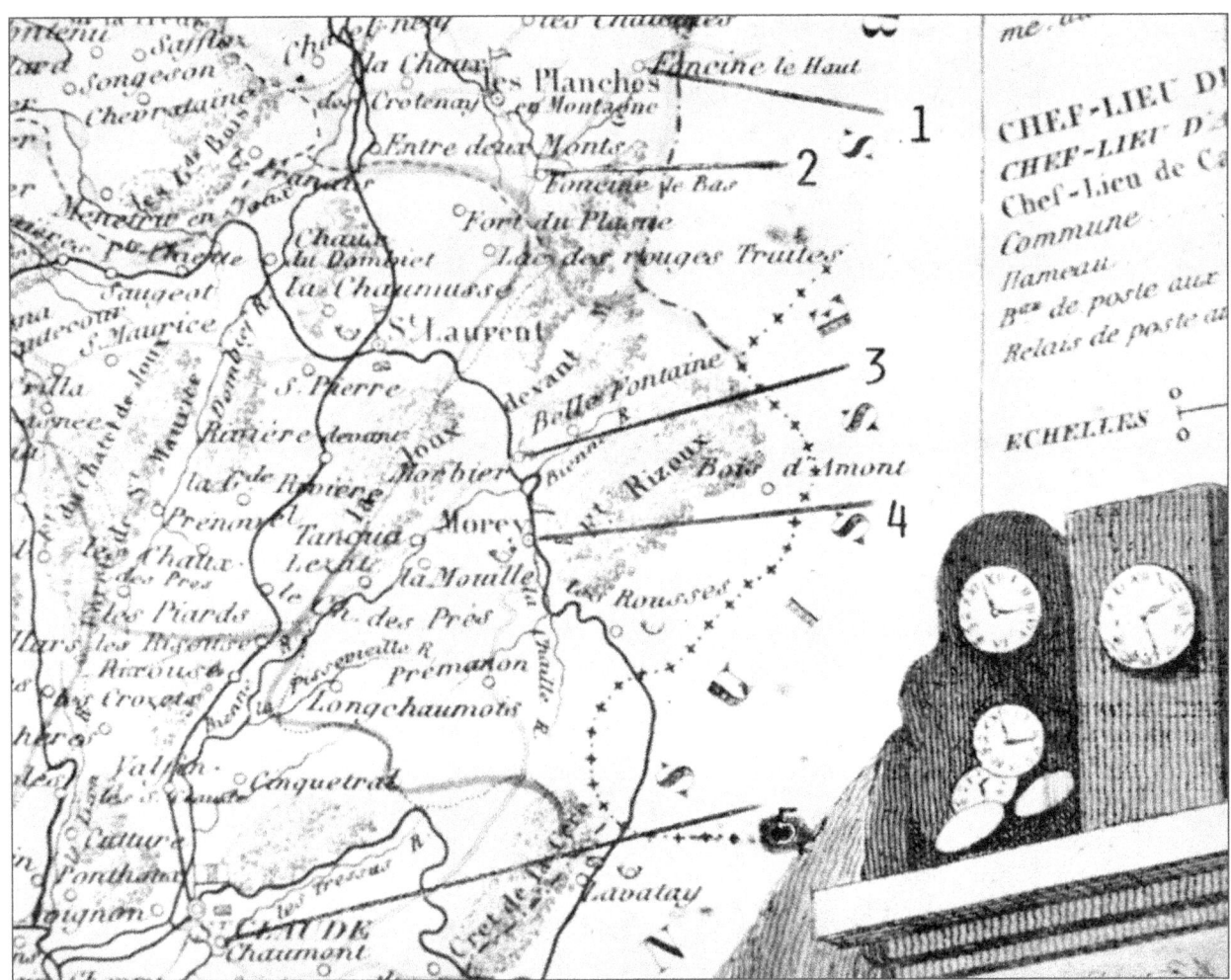

Figure 3. Map of Jura showing principal roads as of 1850. The distance by modern road from Morez (here spelled Morey) to Geneva is only 35 miles, but crosses two ridges, which must have been formidable obstacles in earlier times. This map is from a French atlas of 1850 and is surrounded by pictures of products of the area, hence the clocks to the right.

Behind the dial is a simple robust mechanism (Figure 2) that seemingly will never wear out and that is easily cleaned and put in order. Mounted in an iron cage or frame are bars that carry the trains. The time train, on the left hand side as you face the clock, has a verge or, in later models, a recoil escapement that drives the central pendulum through a link. The striking train has a straight rack that drops vertically and, after striking the hour, automatically repeats the hour one or two minutes later. Most people find the latter most amusing and useful too, in case they are not sure they heard all the strokes the first time.

Although I had owned and worked on French clocks for more than 20 years, it was not until 1965 that I had an opportunity to get acquainted with the Morbier clock. From 1964 to 1970 I looked at hundreds of different examples and worked on the 20 or so that I bought to illustrate the various stages of development of these clocks. In trying to learn more about the history and development of these clocks, I found that very little has been written. Practically all writers about French clocks, overwhelmed by the creations of the famous clockmakers of Paris, found no space left for the humble Morbiers. In this writing I want to share with others what I have learned about this clock, which I like to think of as the Model "T" of European clocks. The mechanism is ruggedly made of easily obtained materials; it was produced in relatively large numbers, and sold at a price that brought it within the reach of many who could not otherwise afford a clock, and it could be kept in running order in rural areas, far from the specialized talents of the big city mechanics.

These notes should be considered as only a beginning, and I hope that others who have knowledge or experience of these clocks will comment on or add to them. In this way, eventually we all will have a better understanding of the how, where, and when of these interesting clocks.

Where Do They Come From?

The name Morbier is derived from the little village in the Haut-Jura (Figure 3), where the production of these clocks was centered for more than 200 years from the early eighteenth century up to the beginning of World War I. These clocks are also known as Comtoise clocks since this part of the Jura lies in the region known as the Franche-Comte, control of which had been disputed since Roman times by the Gauls, Romans, various German tribes and later Austria, Spain, the dukes of Burgundy, and the kings of France. This area is close to the Swiss border. By modern roads it is only about 35 miles from Geneva and about 275 miles southeast of Paris.

Today, the village of Morbier and the adjacent larger town of Morez seem just like a hundred other villages and towns of France. When one sees them today one wonders why, 200 years ago, they suddenly burst into activity and became the center of a cottage-type industry that produced hundreds of thousands of clocks for the ordinary household, which were so durable that a surprising number still exist today. To answer this question I looked into the geography and history of the area and found at least part of the answer.

In the mid-eighteenth century the country around Morbier and Morez was essentially rural; exploitation of the forests and dairy farming furnished the livelihood for the majority of the inhabitants. Even today, if you mention the word "Morbier" to Frenchmen, most of them will think of a particularly fine cheese made in that area and not of clocks. The area was heavily forested, so there was plenty of wood to make charcoal needed for iron making, and there were deposits of iron and limestone. These elements, combined with water power, made it feasible to set up iron furnaces and forges in the valleys. Water mills powered the bellows and the trip hammers, which produced bars and plates of iron and semisteel. Finished products included wire, nails, carriage axles, and agricultural implements. In some areas wrought iron grillwork reached a high state of development. At Besaneon and Lons-le-Saunier there are examples of this work that equal the best in the world. The area around Morbier was noted particularly for the production of scythes and sickles. The operators of the furnaces and forges were always interested in expanding their markets and thus were glad to offer assistance and technical advice to the early clockmakers in the area.

Contrary to the first impression, therefore, in reality all the elements were present for developing a light industry such as clockmaking: raw materials of wrought iron, steel, and wood; skills in the form of blacksmiths and makers of agricultural and household implements; and a supply of labor—farmers and woodsmen who needed employment part of the year. The market would be developed among the farmers and townspeople remote from the big cities who needed a simple dependable clock that was not too expensive and could be kept in repair by the local merchant or the itinerant clockmaker.

How Did They Get Started?

One might say that clockmaking started in this area because of its isolation from the centers of commerce and industry such as Geneva, Paris, Lyon, or Marseilles. According to tradition, about 1660 a monastery clock at St. Claude (No. 5 on map, Figure 3), a nearby religious center dating from the Middle Ages, needed repair, and a blacksmith and wrought iron worker of Morbier (Mayet or Maillet by name) was called in to fix it, since no clockmakers could be found in the area. Finding the clock worn beyond repair, he built a new one by using the old parts as models. This was a success and the blacksmith and his brothers built other public clocks[1] and even began to build simplified versions for interior use. News of the application of the pendulum to clocks finally reached the Jura in 1675, about 20 years after it had been demonstrated by Huygens in the Netherlands. After some experimentation the Mayet brothers succeeded in building a successful pendulum clock for household use, and the "Morbier" was born.

The brothers soon separated, one staying in Morbier (No. 3 on Figure 3), another settling in Bellefontaine, and the third at Foncine-le-Haut (No. 1 on Figure 3). These towns still exist, although there is little evidence of clockmaking there today. On the other hand, at the time of this writing a very active dealer was located at Foncine-le-Bas (No. 2 on Figure 3), who also had an outstanding collection of Morbier clocks that he has gathered during the past 20 years.

How Old Are They?

Sooner or later these questions arise: How old is this clock? How does it fit into the pattern of development? Definitive answers to these questions are not always possible, and the more one learns about these clocks, the more hesitant one becomes to give a simple unequivocal answer. In an attempt to fit the developments of 200 years into some kind of frame of reference, however, I have divided them into three main periods as shown in the accompanying chart. It should be realized, of course, that we are dealing with continuous change in a number of elements so that the limits of these periods cannot be fixed with precision.

The Early Morbier

The first or early Morbier began in the late seventeenth century and phased out about the middle of the eighteenth century. During the earlier part of this period the various elements that later were combined in the Morbier were being introduced, and only individual models are found; no two are exactly alike. Thus, you may find movements with the striking train behind the time train as in the lantern clocks, with anchor escapement or verge, count wheel or rack strike, a brass or pewter dial, usually with a single hand. The posted cage or frame is independent of the bars that carry the trains and are usually fastened in the frame with wedges and no screws.

Figure 4 shows one of these earlier model Morbiers with one hand. The time train is on the left with a recoil escapement and central pendulum suspended by a thread at the rear. On the back of the hour wheel can be seen the 12-pointed star that releases the strike train as in one-hand lantern clocks. This wheel also carries the snail for the rack strike, which is intermediate between the Morbier rack strike and the ordinary

Figure 4. A clock of the early period that has some features of the Morbier.

French or English pivoted rack strike. In this model there is a pivoted rack, but the gathering pawl operates on one side and the rack hook on the other side as in the later Morbiers. The lever and arbor of the independent half-hour strike can be seen on the left. As found, the bell, half-hour strike hammer, and original dial were missing. The ornate cast brass hand is also shown. This clock has a heavy iron loop at the back that was intended to be used to hang the clock on the wall. The stand-off spikes at the bottom are missing

Figure 5. Rearview of early Morbier, showing characteristic features.

Figure 6, right. Pewter dial and ornate cast-brass hand of early Morbier shown in Figure 5. Note alarm disc in form of rosette.

By the end of this period the early Morbier had become fairly standard (Figure 5). It was characterized by a verge escapement, a pear-shaped bob, a pendulum beating seconds or longer, mounted at the back of the frame by a thread suspension; the time train was established on the left and both trains wind counterclockwise. They usually have one hand and dials are of brass or of pewter. They were housed in a simple box of sheet iron and were intended to be hung on the wall or supported by a bracket. These clocks bear many of the marks of handwork, much of it resembling locksmith work. The use of screws is minimal; one finds instead mounting bars fastened by wedges or keys, dovetails, notches, etc. Screws, when used, are primitive, coarse-threaded, and the slots are definitely V-shaped and not straight-sided as they are later. These early Morbiers have little in the way of decoration. The single hand is often ornate, however, and there may be scrolls of thin brass riveted on the iron case, some of which are pivoted and cover the winding holes. Figure 6 is the front view of the early Morbier seen in Figure 5 showing the pewter dial and other traits. This one bears the name of Morteau, a town some 40 miles away from Morbier.

The Bronze-Front Morbier

Later the scroll designs mentioned above were worked in cast brass or bronze, and the fronton became quite prominent. We thus move into the bronze-front Morbier. The earliest ones dating from 1750 are surmounted by a cock or the sun; this was later replaced by eagles during the time of Napoleon. The

Figure 7. Bronze-front Morbier, dating most likely from the French Revolution (1789-1793).

emblem in the center was usually the fleur-de-lis during the days of the monarchy, but this changed first to the clasped hands during the Revolution and later to the Phrygian cap on a pike during the Directoire period (1795-1799).

Figure 7 shows one of these clocks, which has the cock and just below the clasped hands motif. This clock has a decorated enameled dial with a depressed center and ornate wrought iron hands. There are also quite prominent Arabic numerals for each five minutes outside the hour numerals. Also seen are the small pear-shaped lead pendulum bob and the jointed wire pendulum "rod" characteristic of the Morbiers of this period.

Figure 8 shows another bronze-front Morbier with the cock and the Phrygian cap on a pike first used during the Directoire period.

The designs of these cast bronze fronts were continued long after they were first introduced, however, and cannot be relied on to identify the date at which a given clock was made. In some instances it is obvious that the fleur-de-lis, a mark of royalty, has been effaced by a file to salvage the castings (or improve the chances of survival of the owner), but one cannot tell what the relation of this act was either to the date of making or selling the clock or to the date of 1793 when Louis XVI went to the guillotine.

Mechanically, the bronze-front Morbier is little changed from the early Morbier. The posts of the posted frame are a little lighter and the movements are somewhat larger overall. Screws are used in place of wedges, and there is evidence of production in small lots rather than individually. The detents and lifting levers are nicely designed and frequently have fretwork or fancy curlicues that give a certain charm to these functional parts.

In this period we find a great variety of mechanical features; alarms and calendar mechanisms are introduced and quarter-striking on two, three, or four bells. Some models repeat the hour with the quarter and have a chain to repeat the hour at will, a useful feature before the days of electric lights or luminous paint. Tardy, in his book *La Pendule Francaise,* shows a number of these more elaborate Morbier clocks.

Clockmaking in the Franche-Comte profited by political and religious troubles in other parts of Europe. Thus, during the early eighteenth century many skilled workmen from Switzerland, especially Geneva, fled across the mountains and added their talents to those of the native craftsmen. During the French Revolution, Antide Ianvier, born just over the mountain in the town of Gex, who had become clockmaker to Louis XVI, found it expedient to take refuge in this area and raised considerably the level of technology during his stay. The era of the Napoleonic Wars had a negative influence, however, as most of the artisans who had been making clocks were either in the army or were diverted to making weapons used by Napoleon's armies all over Europe.

With the return of peace in 1815, trade and manufacturing were reestablished and the golden age of Morbier clocks begins. By this time production of clocks by "cottage industry" was well organized. In this system a "factor" would obtain the raw materials, establish a standard design, and then put out the materials to families in the neighborhood to make the parts. Each family specialized in certain parts or processes, cutting wheels or pinions, making the cage or frame, fitting the parts together and finally putting the clock in running order. Each of these specialists acquired the equipment or machinery to do his particular task. Some of this machinery was quite advanced and from this period on, the clocks lack the handmade look of the earlier models. The parts, although fairly uniform,

Figure 8. Detail of bronze-front Morbier, showing cock (rooster) and the Phrygian cap on a pike (at arrow), first used during the period of the Directoire (1794-1799).

are not necessarily interchangeable from one clock to another. It was the task of the *rhabilleur* to select the parts that would go together and adjust them to make a working clock. On market day, the finished work was taken to town and traded for food, supplies, and raw materials for the next week's work. The factor then either shipped out the finished clocks to markets in the cities and towns as far as Brittany, Picardy, or Provence or arranged to have itinerant clockmakers peddle them from village to village. Thus, at the same time the Yankee clockmakers were peddling in America, their counterparts

Figure 9, right. Early brass-front clock, showing stylized figures in low relief, with overall geometric pattern. This is a three-train, three-bell, quarter-strike.

were active in France. One reason the pendulum rod on the older Morbier clocks was jointed was to make it easier for the peddler to carry a supply in his pack.

When the road system was organized, the town of Morbier found itself on the main road between Paris and Geneva (see map, Figure 3), which led to its becoming the center for exporting clocks from other parts of the Franche-Comte as well as the local products to Switzerland and to the rest of France. Morbier and Morez still are on the most direct route (Nationale Route No. 5) from Paris to Geneva, but most automobile traffic now takes a somewhat longer route, in miles but not in time, somewhat to the west to take advantage of the superhighway from Paris to Marseilles and avoid some rugged mountain roads.

The Brass-Front Morbier

About 1840 some makers began to substitute pressed brass for the cast bronze front. The earliest of these are in low relief and the design is rather simple and formal. The sun and star motif, horn of plenty, Grecian urn, griffons, or other mythical creatures are most frequently found. A good deal of the area was covered by a simple geometric pattern.

Figures 9 and 10 show two of these early pressed brass fronts. It appears that these fronts were adapted to different size dials by cutting them at the sides and pushing top and bottom together as can be clearly seen in Figure 9. This is seen so often that it must have been a standard practice and not improvisation. The enameled dial is standard, and the Arabic numerals that were quite prominent on the earlier clocks are now quite small and appear only at 15, 30, 45, and 60 minutes. The name and town of the seller begin to appear on the dial and very rarely the name of the maker.

Along with these early brass fronts there were simple bob pendulums seen through a small bull's eye window in the case. Soon, however, these windows were enlarged, and the grille pendulums became common with either a large brass bob or painted glass bob. The grilles were false and it is doubtful that any true compensating pendulums were made. Figure 11 (see page 10) shows two types of grille pendulums from this period.

The movements by this time were quite standardized and most of the marks of hand forging and shaping of parts are no longer found. Screws replaced the wedges and dovetails of earlier models, and the fretwork and curlicues of the detents and other moving pieces that are part of the charm of the bronze front and earlier types have disappeared. The substantial cut gears and pinions remain to the end, however, and apparently no maker dared to cut corners and adopt cheaper methods of manufacture.

Figure 10, right. Embossed brass-front with simple stylized design, typical of early period.

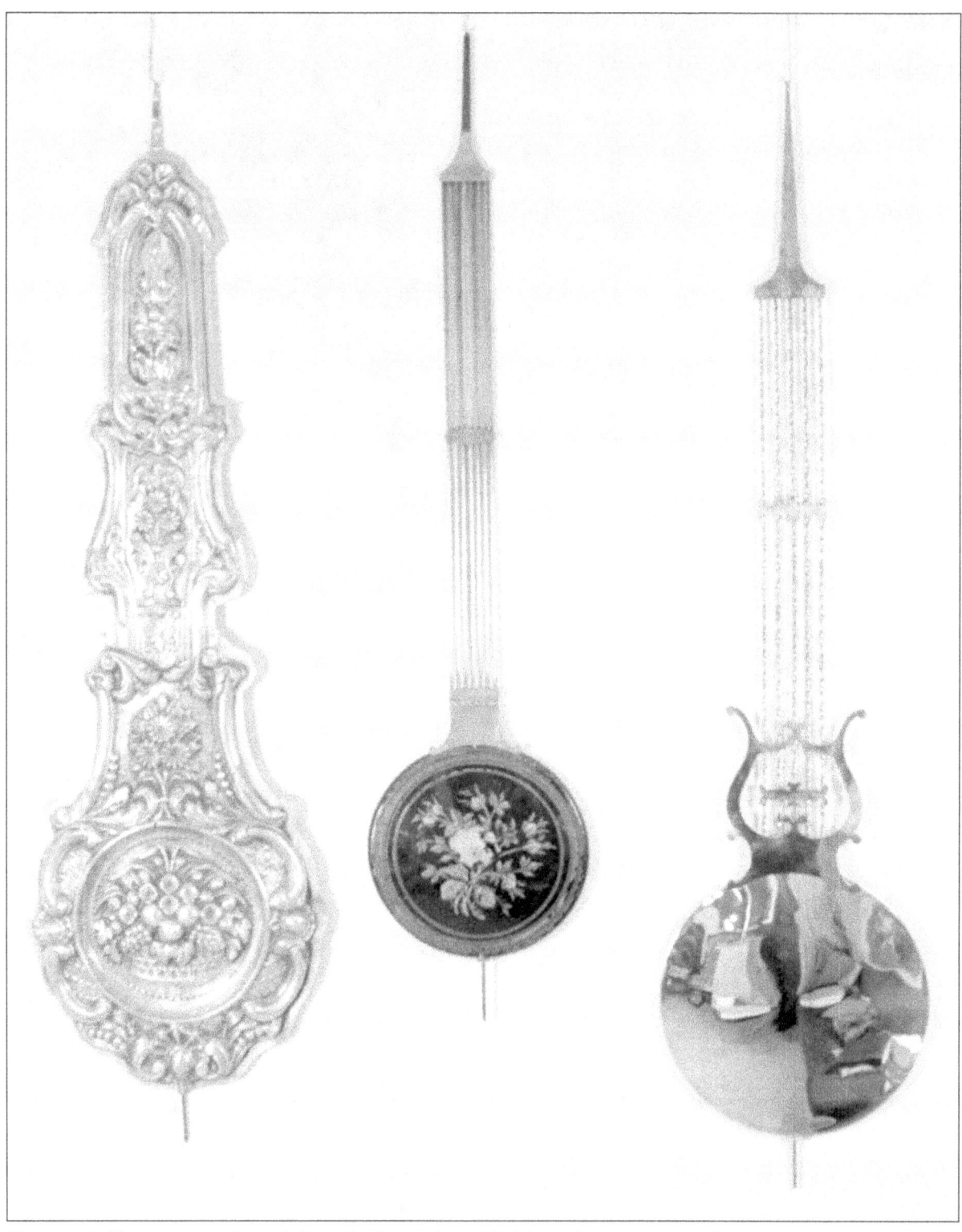

Figure 11. Three types of pendulums for brass-front Morbiers. At center is a false gridiron with painted glass bob, and at the right is the lyre-type; these are both from the earlier period. On the left is an unpainted embossed brass model of the later period.

It was in this period that production reached a level of about 80,000 clocks per year. In 1856 Morez had become a thriving town with some 4,000 inhabitants, 18 factories, 10 foundries for wheels and bells, and 8 makers of enameled dials. It should be understood that factory as used here denotes more of a warehouse for raw materials, intermediate stages, and finished movements than a place where the various operations were carried out. The work was still done on the farms and in the homes of the villagers, principally during the winter, when work in the fields and forests was at a minimum.

Figure 12. Embossed brass pendulum with moving figures of children on a seesaw.

Figure 13. Later brass-front clock with a religious-nautical theme.

The Later Brass Front

By 1860 the bronze front had been completely displaced by the embossed brass front, and the fancy pendulums began to appear. The variety and ingenuity of these pendulums are almost without limit. There are reported to be over 100 designs, most of which were prepared by artist-designers in Paris, but which were executed in the Morbier district. Because of their massive appearance it is quite a shock the first time one handles one of these to discover that the total weight is only about two pounds. The very thin brass is backed up by a flat piece of thin sheet iron. The pendulum on the left in Figure 11 is typical of these, and Figure 12 shows one of these with children on a seesaw that rocks with the movement of the pendulum.

Along with these elaborate pendulums, you find a great variety of subjects in the brass front. The simple stylized designs became more elaborate, and many scenes of domestic life, especially rural, are found. These are worked in high relief, which must have required considerable technical skill to avoid tearing or wrinkling the metal.

Figure 13 shows one with a religious motif with a young man receiving a cross as he is about to set out to sea. The simple pleasures of a picnic in the country are portrayed in the front shown in Figure 1. The clock shown in Figure 18 with two doves in a nest is a so-called "marriage clock" and apparently was a traditional wedding gift in those days. Usually stamped in the border or a corner of the design is the word "brevete" or "depose" (sometimes both), which means that the design was copyrighted or registered.

The mechanical features of these later period Morbiers are noted in the chart on page 12. These are the ones that are most frequently found on the market today. Alarm and calendar clocks are frequently found and more rarely quarter-strike, most of which are the simplified two-train type rather than the more complicated three-train grand sonnerie.

Decline of the Morbier

By the terms of the treaty at the end of the Franco-Prussian War in 1871, German goods were admitted to France practically duty-free, and the cheaper German clocks gave the Morbiers stiff competition. The taste also was changing to smaller clocks and chime clocks so that the market for Morbiers began to decline, particularly after 1890. Some of the more enterprising makers in Morez adapted to these changing tastes and produced the picture frame clocks. These are good-sized wall clocks with a gong strike and a modified Morbier movement with two tremendous springs. Figure 14 shows one of these with an ornate ebonized wooden case inlaid with brass, colored woods, and mother of pearl.

Figure 14. Picture frame clock with modified spring-driven Morbier movement. Overall height is 24 inches.

PRINCIPAL CHARACTERISTICS OF MORBIER CLOCKS IN DIFFERENT PERIODS		
PERIOD	MOVEMENT	CASE, DIAL, AND DECORATION
EARLY MORBIER 1680-1750	Not yet standard Single hand Use of wedges and dovetails to join parts	No case other than sheet iron box Bob pendulum Brass or pewter dial
BRONZE FRONT 1750-1860	Iron post and plate frame Time and strike trains side by side Verge escapement Pendulum at the rear Thread suspension with steeple Use of screws to fasten parts Repeating strike on bell mounted on top of movement Quarter strike on 2, 3, or 4 bells Wooden drums for weight cords	Porcelain enamel dial usually without name but with prominent Arabic numerals for each five minutes Cast bronze front Wrought iron hands in early period Locally made cases of hard wood Pear-shaped bob pendulum or simple lens of brass Pendulum rod of jointed wire or flat strips may be longer than seconds, usually 1¼ seconds (63" approximately)
BRASS FRONT 1840-1915	Frame and train as above Pendulum at the front	Porcelain enameled dial with name of seller (rarely maker) and town Stamped brass hands
Early Period 1840-1880	Verge escapement Thread suspension Bell on top of movement Quarter-strike — 3-train Usually wooden drums	Small numerals for 15, 30, 45, and 60 minutes only Lens shaped brass bobs, jointed strip pendulum rod. Later grilles with brass or glass bobs, or reversed painted glass panels Simple hardwood cases
Later Period 1860-1915	Anchor escapement Slotted suspension spring in small brass fitting Wire gong mounted on wooden sounding board at rear Quarter-strike — 2-train Brass drums for weight cords	No minute numerals Fancy embossed brass pendulums painted with simple colors and later with iridescent blue and purple — sometimes animated figures Decorated pine cases, but locally made hardwood cases also persist

Figure 15 shows the movement of the clock shown in Figure 14. The lever that releases the strike train has been changed to a U-shape to make the movement more compact, but otherwise the clock is a true Morbier-posted frame, trains carried in bars, "ladder"-type rack, and the strike repeated after one minute.

Picture frame clocks are also found with the conventional count wheel strike and the more usual French movement between plates. These can be identified by the winding holes that are closer to the center hole than the Morbiers. If there is any doubt, a quick look inside will settle the matter.

This is the final phase of the Morbier clock, which began more than 200 years before. With changing economic conditions and the development of true factory production, the archaic cottage-type industry could not compete. The factories ceased operation with the beginning of World War I but new Morbiers could be bought as late as 1925 when the prewar stocks were finally exhausted. Some of the old tools and molds can still be found in the area, however, and because of the current revival of interest in these clocks, limited production of the most perishable parts, the fronts and the pendulums, has begun.

Figure 15. Modified spring-driven Morbier escapement (front of clock shown in Figure 14). Note the ladder-type rack and U-shaped strike release lever pivoted in the center of the post on the right.

Cases for Morbier Movements

The dating of a Morbier movement with its associated front and pendulum is a complex matter as indicated above, but establishing the origin and date of the clock cases is still more difficult. One is never sure that the movement and its case were made for each other. Morbier movements are seldom fitted to a particular case but rest unattached on a simple platform inside the upper part of the case. Thus, changing a movement from one case to another was relatively easy.

Because of the problems and expense of shipping, not many clock cases have been brought to the United States from France. Some of the hardwood cases, in particular, are quite handsome, however, and might well be worth the trouble. The following notes can only give a rough idea of where they come from and how they are associated with the movements at different periods.

From the earliest times, movements were enclosed in sheet iron boxes to keep out the dust and sold to the customers, who then either hung them on the wall, directly or on a bracket, or arranged to have a case made by the local cabinetmaker. At the same time in the latter half of the eighteenth century and continuing into the nineteenth century Morbier movements were put in cases, which had originally had other movements that were less satisfactory than the rugged Morbiers. Depending on the resources of the area the cases may be of oak, chestnut, cherry, or walnut. Some of these are quite handsome with molding and carvings in Louis XV and XVI styles.

The style of these cases varied with the area. In Normandy, for example, they developed an amazing variety of individual models using carving and molding, and yet they all fall within an overall formal, rather slender form. In other areas a broader case is found and even before the development of the elaborate pendulums there are cases with curved sides without an opening for the pendulum to be seen.

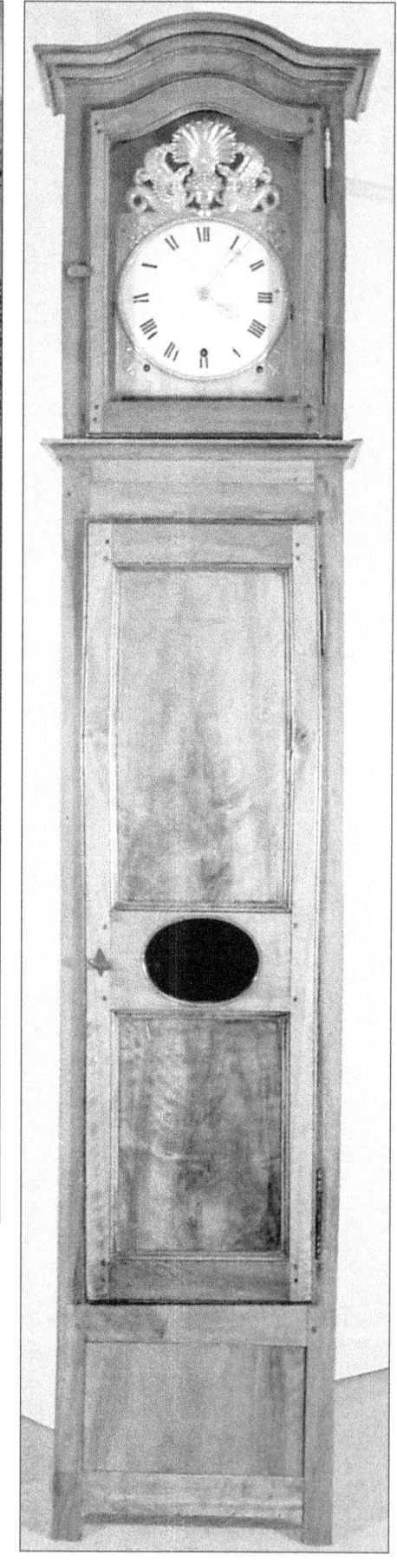

Figure 16, above. Oak case with Morbier movement, most likely from Burgundy. The small lead pendulum bob and articulated rod are barely visible to the right, along the door opening.

Figure 17, right. Simple box-like case of walnut, with movement of early brass-front period.

Figure 16 shows a bronze-front movement (also shown close-up in Figure 7), in an oak case with Louis XV style carvings and moldings. This case design is characteristic of Burgundy and was recently brought to the Paris area from Dijon, the capital of Burgundy, which is about 100 miles northwest of Morbier. The movement and the case seem to be contemporary and probably have been together since made.

Figure 17 shows a plain case in walnut. The joinery is simple and straightforward, with rugged mortise-and-tendon joints and no attempt to hide the wooden pins. The case was originally quite high and has been cut down to seven feet six inches to make it more suitable for modern houses. There is some uncertainty as to whether the movement found with this case has been with it from the beginning. This movement is of the early brass-front period and bears the name of Valence, which is today a good-sized city in the Rhone Valley about 200 miles from Morbier. Walnut was available as a wood for cabinetmaking in nearby Savoy, so it was plausible that this was sold by a dealer in Valence and that he or the buyer had a case made by a local joiner. Some doubt is thrown on this, however, because the pendulum is suspended from the back of this movement and is barely visible through the small window. Therefore, the case may have been made for a later model Morbier with a flat brass bob suspended from the front of the movement.

Figure 18, above. Plain cherry case from Brittany, with late brass-front Morbier movement.

Figure 19, right. Pine case with imitation wood graining and naive hand-painted decorations.

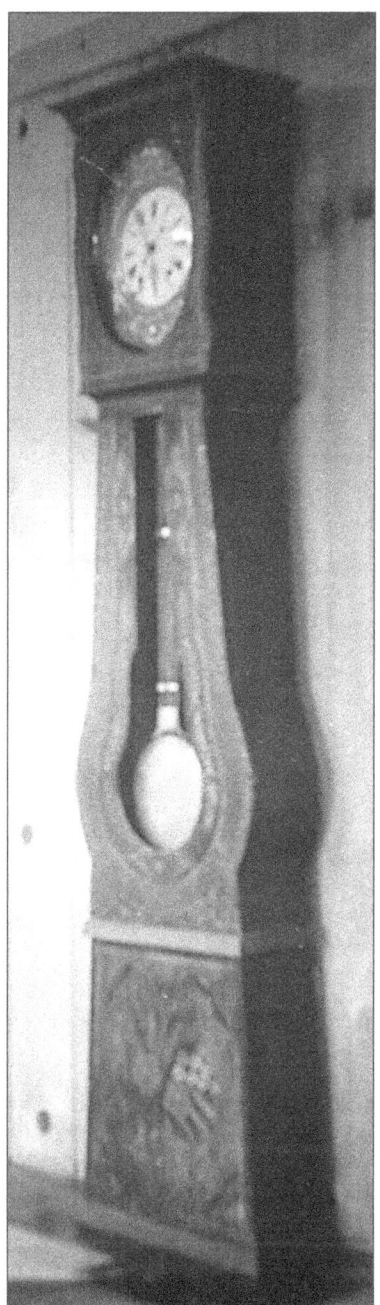

Figure 18 is a close-up of a plain case of cherry with a beautiful figured grain. The movement is a late brass front bearing the name of the town Becherel, a village in Brittany about 250 miles west of Paris and more than 500 miles from Morbier. The movement fits the case very well and is believed to be original.

After the railroads reached Morez about 1860, it became practical to make cases in the area and ship them out by rail with the movements. This coincided with the introduction of the elaborate pendulums that required a broader case. With simple directness they merely broadened out the lower part of the straight-sided case into the characteristic shape so often seen in cartoons showing French clocks (Figure 19). These cases were made of pine and decorated in a rather primitive manner with artificial graining and designs produced by applying a coat of paint and then scraping it off while still wet with the fingers or simple scrapers to produce the design (as in finger painting). The flat areas were also decorated with flower designs painted by hand. Nearby towns such as Les Rousses and Champagnole became centers for casemaking, which were made in the homes of the farmers and villagers; women and girls did most of the decorating.

THE TIME TRAIN

The previous chapter gave an overall view of the Morbier clock with some indication of the development of the mechanism and the cases over its 200-year history. This section gives further details of the time train with particular emphasis on the verge or crown wheel escapement that is found on most of the clocks built up to about 1880 and brief treatments of the more familiar anchor escapement used in later years and the pinwheel escapement, which is found occasionally.

The Verge Escapement

For most people the verge escapement is something they had read about many years ago when they first became interested in clocks or watches. Any history usually shows at least one picture of an early clock of the fifteenth or sixteenth century with a foliot balance and mentions its poor accuracy. Such books quickly move on to the pendulum clock and to anchor and deadbeat escapements and leave one with the impression that verge escapements were quickly supplanted by these later developments. Collectors of European watches, on the other hand, know that the verge escapement was used in thousands of watches well into the nineteenth century.

Therefore, it comes as a surprise when one sees a verge escapement in a Morbier clock, the first impulse is to think that one has stumbled onto a really early clock of the fifteenth or sixteenth century (Figure 20).

Most likely, however, the clock is little more than a hundred years old, although in some cases it may date from the time of the French Revolution or earlier. Some hints on establishing the date of these clocks were given in earlier paragraphs.

The second idea one has of the verge escapement, namely, that it is fundamentally inaccurate, is also very likely to be abandoned after one has observed such a clock for several weeks or months. In modern American houses where the temperature remains fairly constant, this weight-driven clock is surprisingly accurate and will keep time with all but the best regulators. It is not often recalled that Harrison's chronometer No. 4, with which he eventually won the Admiralty award, was essentially a big watch with a verge escapement and temperature compensation. Although later chronometers used more advanced (and more delicate) escapements, Harrison proved that with superior craftsmanship and attention to detail the verge escapement could perform as well as the more complicated mechanisms.

Nevertheless, the verge escapement in lantern clocks had serious weaknesses when used with the short pendulum. During the seventeenth and eighteenth centuries there was a great deal written about the strengths and weaknesses of the verge escapement, which at that time, was practically the only one available for use in watches. In almost all instances these early writers recognized that friction during recoil was the real enemy in verge escapements in watches and most clocks of the

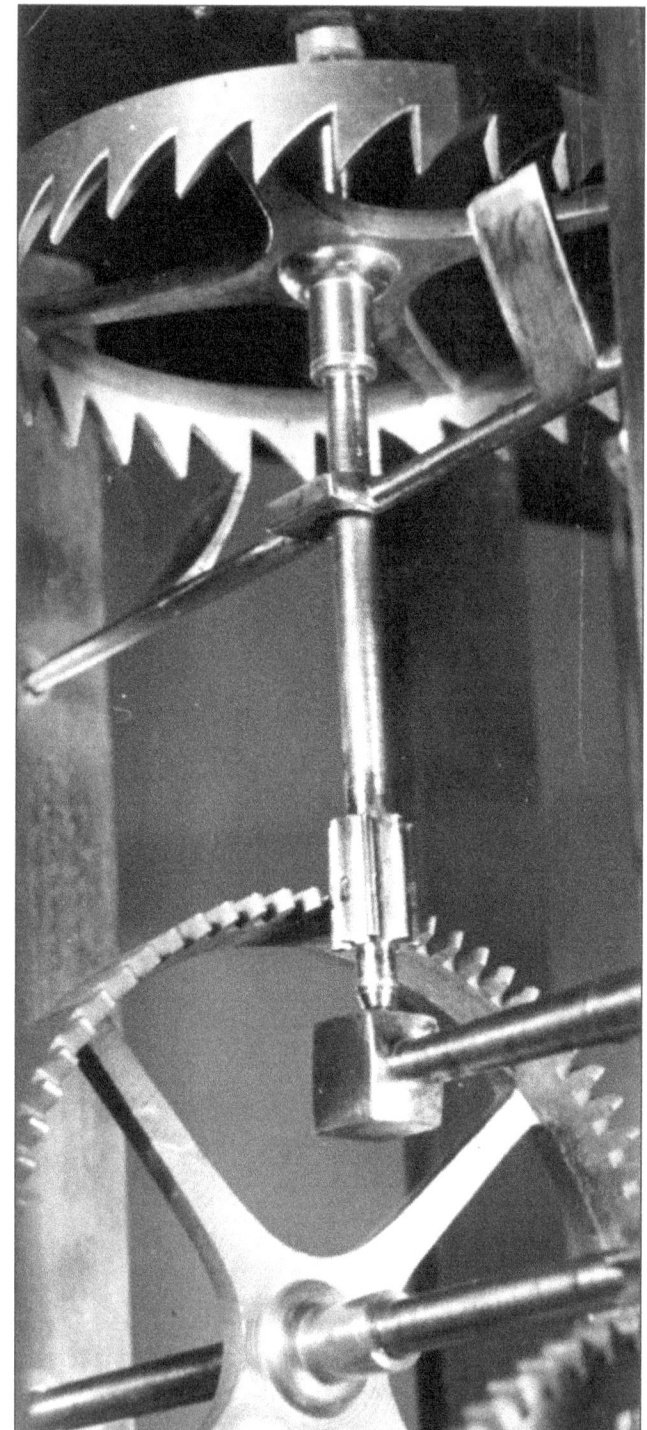

Figure 20. The verge escapement as found in the classic Morbier from about 1750 to 1880.

period. A study of the accompanying diagrams reveals why this is so and shows how the design of the escapement in Morbier clocks overcomes this defect to a great extent.

Figure 21 is a diagram of the verge escapement used in lantern clocks after the introduction of the pendulum. The portion to the right of the center line in these schematic drawings represents the part of the wheel and the pallet in front, whereas the shaded part on the left represents the pallet and part of the escape wheel behind. In this sketch tooth (a) has just escaped from pallet (A) as the verge and the pendulum swing in a counterclockwise direction and tooth (b) has dropped on pallet (B) which, still moving in a counterclockwise direction, causes the escape wheel to recoil to the left against the force of the train which impels it to the right. The line along which the pressure of the escape wheel acts to resist can be seen to be at an angle of about 40 degrees with a perpendicular to the surface of the pallet. The relatively short length and wide angle of the pallets mean that there is considerable friction and wear when the movement of the pendulum causes the escape wheel to recoil.

Figure 22 shows the proportions of the verge escapement usually found in the Morbier clocks and indicates the relation of the parts at the beginning of recoil. The force acts at an angle of about 20 degrees with the perpendicular to the surface of the pallet or half that shown in Figure 22. The Morbier clocks have longer pallets in proportion to the depth of engagement in the escape wheel, a smaller angle between the pallets, and curved working faces of the pallets that bring them more nearly perpendicular to the plane of rotation of the escape wheel teeth. As a result there is less relative motion of the escape wheel teeth with respect to the pallet, and wear and friction are reduced more than in the lantern clock escapement.

The dimensions of a typical lantern clock of about 1700 and a Morbier of perhaps 1800 are compared in Table I.

As far as I have been able to determine verge escapements with such proportions were used only in Morbier clocks.[3] Apparently, the French theoreticians of the mid-eighteenth century were no longer interested in the verge escapement for clocks, and it was left to the practical clockmakers of the Jura to work things out independently. Outside of France, only relatively short pallets requiring a large amplitude of the pendulum were used.

Another unusual feature of the Morbier clock is that it combines a verge escapement with a long pendulum beating seconds or even longer in a relatively narrow case. Lantern clocks using verge escapements have short pendulums either directly mounted on the verge or, when they are driven by a crutch, the suspension spring is essentially coaxial with the verge so the arc of the pendulum is the same as that of the verge. This is a disadvantage because of the circular error in large arcs of the pendulum. Various devices were developed before the invention of the anchor escapement to reduce the arc of the pendulum while retaining the verge escapement. For example, Huygens developed a gearing arrangement, and in the so-called Zaandam clocks there is another system using a vertical verge and a horizontal rod that is linked to the pendulum at about one-third its length so that the arc of the verge is greater than the arc of the pendulum.

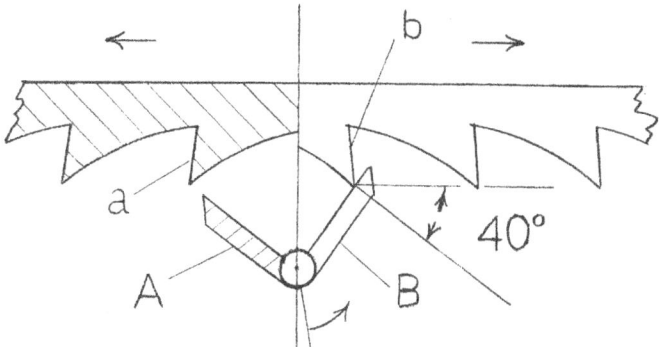

Figure 21, left. Verge escapement used in lantern clocks and bracket clocks 1650-1750 (shown inverted for comparison with Figure 22).

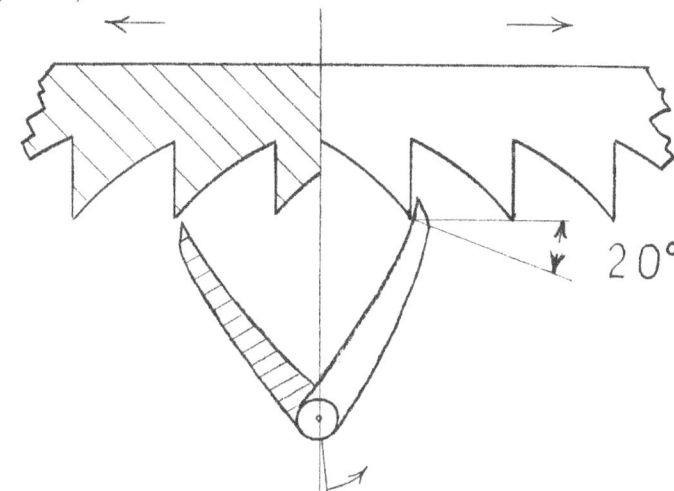

Figure 22. Verge escapement used in Morbier clocks 1750-1880.

TABLE I		
	Lantern Clock	**Morbier**
Diameter of escape wheel	35.0 mm	55.0 mm
Number of teeth	15	31
Distance between teeth	7.5 mm	5.5 mm
Angle between pallets	90°	58°
Length of pallets	6.0 mm	13.5 mm
Depth of pallets in escape wheel	2.0 mm	1.8 mm
Ratio of depth to length of pallets	1:3	1:7.5

In the earlier Morbier clocks the "steeple" that carries the thread suspension is quite high, sometimes as much as four inches above the top plate of the frame. With the linking arrangement used in the Morbier clocks this means that the arc of the verge is greater than the arc of the pendulum since the radius of the former is less. For example, in the clock shown in Figure 28, the distance from the thread suspension to the pivot for the horizontal link is 9-1/2 inches, whereas the distance from the pallet arbor pivot to the link is about 3-1/2 inches. Thus, the arc of the verge is nearly three times the arc of the pendulum.

In later models the height of the steeple was reduced, but even after the pendulum was moved to the front, they still retained a difference in height of the respective centers so that the arc of the pendulum was less than that of the verge (Figure 23).

By means of this arrangement, together with a jointed pendulum rod, the makers of Morbier clocks achieved a unique and practical solution to the problem of combining a long pendulum having a small arc of oscillation with a verge escapement.

While most historians of clockwork do not seem to have been aware of the Morbier clocks, Drummond Robertson in his *Evolution of Clockwork* has a note that pinpoints the essential characteristics. In his treatment of Zaandam clocks, he has a footnote as follows: "A somewhat similar arrangement was, however, perpetuated in the clocks made in the Franche Comte in France until the middle of the nineteenth century; but in these the crown wheel was set with the teeth pointing downwards, and very long pallets were employed. The long pendulum itself swung behind the dial. They seemed to be excellent timekeepers."[4]

With the development after 1850 of the broad pendulums of repousse brass, which were rigid except at the point where they were attached to the upper pendulum rod, there was an incentive to reduce the arc still further, and a trend began away from the verge to the anchor escapement. While adapted to

Figure 23, left. Overall view of the time train of a late model Morbier with verge escapement.

Figure 24, right. Side view of same movement, showing heavy cut wheels and high count pinion.

the cottage-type industry, the fabrication of the verge, the crown wheel, and the contrate wheel was more complicated and expensive than the corresponding anchor, flat escape wheel, and the third wheel. In addition, a separate support for the crown wheel was not needed in the anchor escapement. The production of Morbier clocks with verge escapements gradually gave way to the anchor and for all practical purposes came to an end in the 1870s.

The Time Train

Figures 23 and 24 show the time train only of a typical Morbier with verge escapement made during the mid-nineteenth century. As noted earlier, the train is carried in wrought iron bars with brass inserts in which the pivots turn. The train consists of the barrel and three wheels each of which functions somewhat differently from those in an English or American weight-driven clock. The second wheel turns once in two hours rather than once an hour as does the center wheel in most clocks. The arbor of this wheel drives the motion wheel and pinion through a leaf spring. These in turn drive the minute hand and hour hand, respectively. This system permits the time train to be at one side of the frame and drive the hands without any additional wheels. It also makes it possible to use a high count pinion on the second wheel arbor where the stress is greatest.

The third wheel is a contrate wheel that drives the escape wheel pinion mounted vertically. The escape wheel arbor is carried by a simple brass cock at the top, but the lower end is supported by a turned arm that is threaded and fastened in the upright bar with a nut (see Figure 20). The other end is drilled to receive the lower end of the escape wheel arbor. Usually, this hole is blind and acts as a thrust bearing to take the weight of the escape wheel.

The depth of the pallets in the escape wheel in such clocks can be regulated by bending this arm. Figure 25, however, shows a threaded brass screw in the support arm that can be turned to adjust the depth.

In early model Morbiers one may find the verge above the escape wheel in the same form as it appears in lantern clocks. In most Morbier clocks, however, the escape wheel is inverted (i.e., the teeth point downward and act on the verge that is mounted underneath).

TABLE II

	Verge	Anchor
Main wheel	96	96
Second wheel pinion	14	14
Second wheel	84	90
Third wheel pinion	8	8
Third wheel	72	82
Escape wheel pinion	7	8
Escape wheel	31	31
Motion work pinion	16	15
Motion work wheel	72	72
Hour hand wheel	96	90
Minute hand wheel	36	36

For the clock shown in Figures 23 and 24 the wheel and pinion counts are shown in the left-hand column of Table II.

This gearing corresponds to 1,674 beats per hour, which would require a simple pendulum 1.15 meters or 45.25 inches long. The upper pendulum rod is carried by a thread in the little sheet iron steeple and has a loop to pass around the hour hand cannon as in American banjo or lyre clocks. In this particular clock it is 11-1/4 inches long from the top loop, which is shaped like a shepherd's crook, to the hole at the lower end. The lower, jointed, pendulum rod is 39 inches from the end of the threaded end to the hook at the upper end. The bob is 6-1/4 inches in diameter and weighs about 6 ounces. It can be adjusted so that its center will be approximately 45 inches from the thread suspension to give the required number of beats. The more elaborate pendulums characteristic of the later brass-front Morbiers are from 41 inches to 43 inches long or about 52 inches to 54 inches overall to give the same number of beats because of the distribution of the mass along the pendulum rod.

In this clock the verge measures 12 centimeters (4.7 inches) from the pivot to the link while the upper pendulum rod measures 19 centimeters (7.5 inches) from the thread suspension to the point where the verge link attaches. Thus, the ratio of the arc of the pendulum rod to the arc of the verge is about 6 to 10.

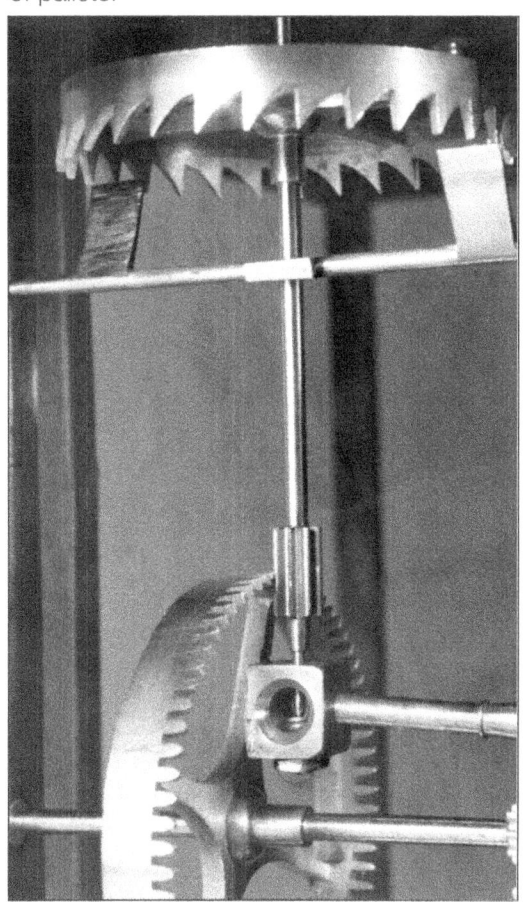

Figure 25. Close-up of escapement, showing curved pallets and screw to adjust depth of pallets.

The diameter of the drum is 1-7/16 inches, which with the wheel counts shown, gives a weight drop of about 8 inches per day or 64 inches for the usual eight days. The weights are cast iron and weigh from 6 to 8 pounds each. Earlier ones were "streamlined" as in Figure 26 on the right, presumably to avoid interference with the pendulum or the case. One frequently finds in Morbier clocks a hard twisted weight cord of a deep red color, which fades with age to pink. This is characteristic of late model brass-front clocks, which were originally mounted in a decorated pine case with the elaborate repousse brass pendulum. Many of these cases were lined with red cotton flannel, and the cords were also dyed red probably to make them less apparent. It is possible to buy this red cord in various weights even in France. Most people are turning to braided nylon cord, however, which is certainly practical, although anachronistic.

One feature of the verge escapement should be emphasized. Despite the obvious motion and friction of the escape wheel and pallets, they should never be oiled. Because of the form of the pallets it is almost impossible to maintain a reasonable film of oil where it is needed. When it dries and collects dust, the pallets wear very quickly. But clocks that have run a hundred years with no oil on the pallets show practically no wear while others that have been recently worked on and oiled by clockmakers unfamiliar with this aspect of the verge escapement may have deeply grooved pallets.

The foregoing paragraphs describe the "classic" Morbier with verge escapement made in great numbers during the nineteenth century and that are most often found on the market. From time to time, however, one may find an earlier model; the following notes may assist in identifying such a clock.

Earlier Verge Movements

Figure 27 shows the dial and front of a Morbier most likely dating from the period of the French Revolution.

The dial has a concave-convex shape (called *creuse* in French) and the wrought iron hands are hand-finished. Arabic numerals for the minutes are rather large and there is some decoration of the dial, but numerals and design are almost always in black. When you look behind the dial of such a clock, you should find considerable evidence of handwork in the forming of the parts. Figure 28 is the rearview of this same clock, which shows the following characteristics:

1. Rather high steeple (4-5 inches) for the thread suspension at the back of the clock.
2. Light crossings on the wheels.
3. Curlicue on the strike detent.
4. Forged link between verge and upper pendulum rod rather than brass strip.
5. The "feet" of the vertical bars are rather small, and sometimes the bars are perfectly straight with no "feet."

Figure 26. Streamlined weight on right; later style on left.

Figure 27. Dial of verge escapement Morbier dating from 1790 to 1795. Note wrought iron hands and medallion where fleur-de-lis have been partially filed off.

Figure 29 is a close-up of the escapement showing:
1. A lighter escape wheel than is found in later models.
2. Light pallets and nicely wrought verge.
3. Nicely turned lower support for the escape wheel.
 A comparison of these details with those of the later models shown in Figures 20, 23, 24, and 25 will reveal the differences.

Figure 29. Escapement of earlier Morbier shown in Figure 27. Note lighter escape wheel and pallets.

Figure 28. General view of movement of clock shown in Figure 27. Note lightness of wheel crossing and escape wheel.

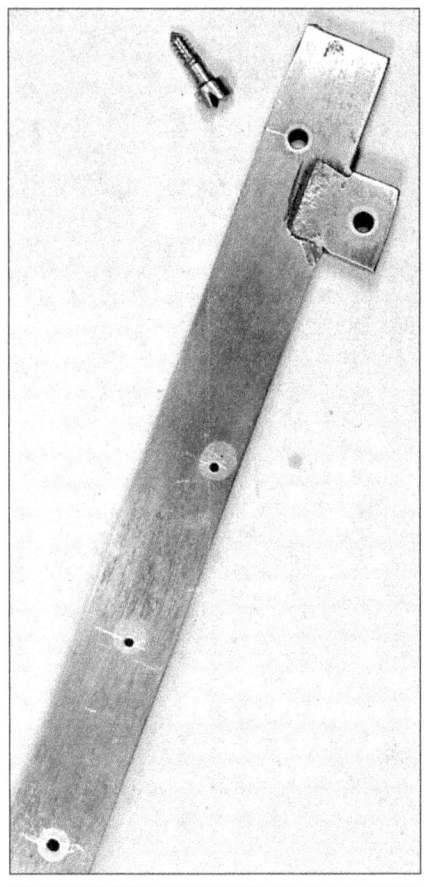

Figure 30, left. V-slotted screw and bar with mortised extension found in early model Morbiers.

Associated with such early model bronze-front Morbiers will be other evidences of handwork such as square head, V-slot screws, and mortises to fabricate parts (Figure 30). Another indication of an earlier Morbier is a mounting for the center arbor made of one piece with the upright bar as in Figure 31. On later models the center arbor is usually carried in a black iron bar that is part of the cage and not removable.

Verge movements with the pendulum at the back usually are associated with the lead bob pendulums and cases with no window through which the pendulum can be seen. The earlier clocks are also likely to have a longer pendulum beating one and a quarter seconds. Later, the pendulum suspension was moved to the front, right behind the dial, so that the lenticular brass bob or the gridiron pendulum could be seen through a small round window or a larger window in the shape of the lyre or grille pendulum.

Month clocks with verge escapements are rarely found. They are quickly recognized by an extra wheel between the main wheel and the arbor that drives the motion work. The winding squares are below the dial rather than in the usual 4 and 8 o'clock positions. The weights, if one is fortunate enough to find them, weigh about 20-25 pounds each.

In dating clocks the most important factor is the overall consistency of the various parts. The dial, front, and hands should be of the same period as the movement. While cast bronze fronts were still being made in the mid-nineteenth century when batch production of movements in considerable quantities had already begun, if you find a bronze front on a movement showing little evidence of hand-finishing, it is much more likely that a bronze front has been relatively recently added to a later model movement.

The Anchor Escapement

Figures 32 and 33 show the general arrangement of the time train of a late model Morbier with anchor escapement. Note that the pendulum is mounted at the front and the thread suspension in a steeple has given way to a slotted suspension spring. As in verge clocks with front mounted pendulums, the upper pendulum rod has a loop to clear the hour hand pipe. The verge also is bent to clear the winding square and is linked to the pendulum rod by a simple brass link. The lengths of the verge and the upper pendulum rod to the link are almost the same since no reduction in arc is needed with the anchor escapement. The motion work and friction spring are similar to those in clocks with verge escapement. The wheel counts are shown in column 2 of Table II (see page 19) and provide for a pendulum with 1,787 beats per hour, which is very close to a second pendulum. Almost invariably in anchor escapement Morbiers there is an escape wheel with 31 teeth. Apparently, the tradition was established with verge escapements and was retained with the anchor where an odd number of teeth is no longer required and is disadvantageous if one wants a second pendulum. The barrel is 1-3/8 inches in diameter so the weight falls about 7-1/2 inches per day or 60 inches in eight days.

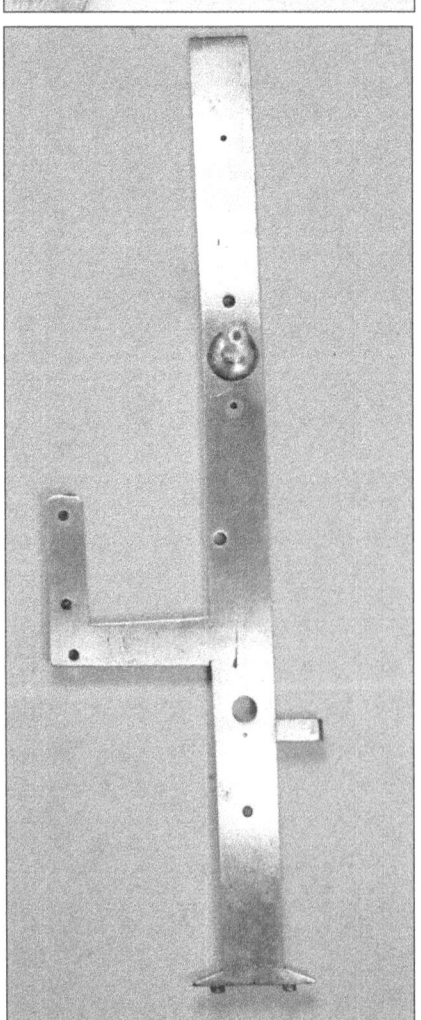

Figure 31, left. Rearview of front bar of time train of early Morbier clock, with mortised and forged support for center arbor; note small foot.

Figure 32. General view of time train of late model Morbier with anchor escapement.

Figure 33. Side view of time train.

Figure 34 is a close-up of the escapement showing the shape of the anchor and escape wheel. The diameter of the escape wheel is 51 millimeter or almost exactly 2 inches. The center-to-center distance between the escape wheel and pallet arbors is 43 millimeter or about 1-11/16 inches. The anchor in most Morbier clocks is of the "gable" form with relatively long pallets embracing about one-quarter of the escape wheel. The entry pallet face is curved, and the exit pallet face is usually straight. The long pallet arms make it relatively easy to open or close the pallets, and there is usually an eccentric bushing for one pivot to permit adjustment of the depth.

The escapement is easy to repair because the parts are substantial and there is plenty of material to work on if the pallets are worn or the wheel needs to be trued. The pivots are generous so that one practically never has to rebush the holes.

The thread suspension is replaced by a rather substantial suspension spring mounted in a brass block at the top of the frame. The upper pendulum rod is usually just long enough so that the hole for the pendulum hook is below the frame so that it can be easily seen when attaching the pendulum. When mounted in the case, the rod swings free but when placed on the bench for repairs, the pendulum rod is lifted and would bend or break the suspension spring if rigidly mounted with pins as in other clocks. To avoid this, one of the brass mountings for the suspension spring is elongated and has a triangular slot that is just long enough to allow the pendulum rod to rise until it is flush with the bottom plate of the frame.

Figure 35 shows three models of such suspension springs to assist those who may have to make one to replace one that is missing. Other models have a safety feature in the form of a hood with slots that engage an extra long and heavy pin in the upper pendulum rod when it is lifted and thus avoid any strain on the suspension spring.

The Pinwheel Escapement

Morbier clocks were also fitted with pinwheel escapements of the type invented by Amant in 1741 and improved by LePaute. Although found occasionally in regular striking clocks for household use, they are more common in regulators without strike mechanism and in clocks intended to drive outside dials as in shops or the town halls of innumerable villages in France. The latter are usually larger in size and have correspondingly large weights to overcome the friction, wind, and possibly ice and snow encountered in exposed dials.

Figure 36 is an overall view of such a clock with the drive for the remote dials at the upper left. In Figure 37 (see page 26) the drive has been removed so that the pinwheel escapement can be seen more clearly.

The gearing in this clock is quite unusual in that there is only one wheel between the main wheel and the escape wheel. The counts are shown in Table III.

The motion work arbor turns once in two hours as in the usual Morbier, but instead of being driven at the same speed as the second wheel as in the verge and anchor movements described above, there is a third wheel of 120 teeth mounted fast on the arbor driven by a 12-tooth pinion on the second wheel arbor. Instead of a friction spring, there is a 60-tooth ratchet between the arbor and the motion work wheel and pinion, which ensures a positive drive to the hands but also means that

Figure 34, above. Detail of "gable" anchor. Note curved face of entry pallet and straight face of exit pallet. All moving parts of this clock bear the number 26, indicating (probably) that they were of batch production.

Figure 35, below. At top are three models of slotted suspension springs as used in Morbier clocks; for comparison two other types usually found in French clocks are shown below.

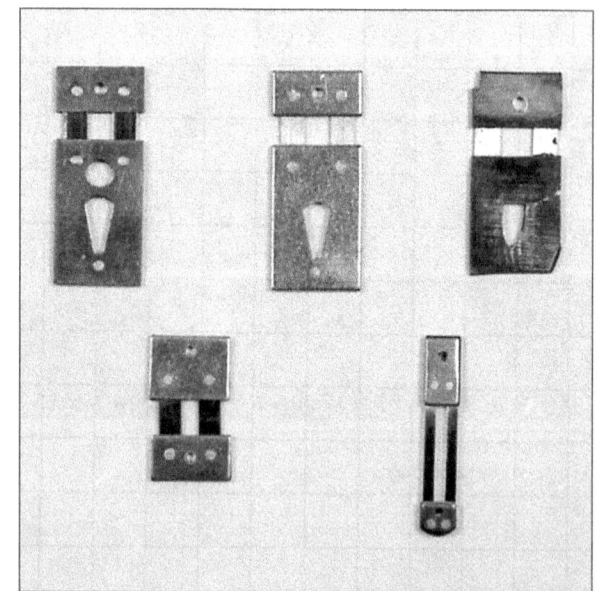

the hands can only be set forward. From a study of Figure 36 and the wheel counts it can be seen that the main wheel also turns once in two hours. This arrangement provides a lot of power to drive the hands but makes frequent winding necessary. The width of the barrel permits 30 turns of the steel cable, so the clock only runs 60 hours and has to be wound every other day. The diameter of the barrel is 2-1/8 inches so that the weight falls about 13 feet in two days or about seven feet if a pulley is used.

The escape wheel is of heavy brass, 62.5 millimeters (2-7/16 inches) in diameter, and the diameter of the "pitch" circle of the pins is 55 millimeters (2-1/8 inches). The distance from the center line of the pallet arbor to the dead face of the shorter pallet is 94.5 millimeters (3-11/16 inches). Thus, the ratio of the length of the pallet arm to the diameter of the escape wheel is about 1.72 to 1. Saunier, in discussing the pinwheel escapement, notes that LePaute had stated the ratio should be 1.5 to 1 as the best compromise. Later theorists believed that the pallet arms should be shorter to reduce friction during the supplementary arc, but this requires greater precision in making the parts and also results in greater sensitivity to wear in the pivots. In more refined French movements of the first half of the nineteenth century, for example, one finds the corresponding ratio to be 1 to 1 or even as little as 0.5 to 1. It is likely that the makers of Morbier clocks with pinwheel escapements chose the longer pallet arms because they realized their standards of accuracy were not very high and they also wanted the clocks to continue to function even though the pivots and pallets were worn.

Figure 36. Overall view of heavy duty Morbier with pinwheel escapement. Drive to remote dial is at upper left.

Table III

	Pinion	Wheel	Motion Work Pinion	Drive Wheel
Main wheel arbor	--	80	--	--
Second wheel arbor	8	72	12	--
Escape wheel arbor	7	31 pins	--	--
Motion work arbor	15	72	--	120
Hour hand cannon	--	90	--	--
Minute hand arbor	36	--	--	--

The escapement in Figure 37 is the basic Amant design and shows none of the refinements of LePaute. The pins are full round, which means a rather large drop. LePaute had realized that the upper half of the pin did no work and reduced the pin to a D shape, which meant that the drop could be less. Later, the lower semicircle was also flattened, making an even more efficient escapement. These later refinements, however, require that the pins be shaped on a wheel-cutting engine after assembly, and it is likely that the makers of Morbier clocks were content with the simpler procedures because they suited their working capabilities and gave satisfactory results.

It is curious that the tradition of 31 teeth in the escape wheel as established in the verge escapement was so strong that they used it even in a pinwheel escapement as well as in the anchor escapement as noted above.

On the other hand, this clock differs from most Morbiers in having a heavy bob weighing about 15 pounds and a rigid pendulum rod fastened to the upper pendulum rod with a steady pin and screw. The total arc of the pendulum is only about 4 inches so that a flexible rod and a light bob would not be advantageous. The pendulum beats 1,580 per hour corresponding to a simple pendulum 1.30 meters (51.14 inches) long.

The foregoing review of the three types of escapements found in Morbier clocks shows that their makers were consistent in making a rugged dependable mechanism. While the labor input was considerable, each task was comparatively simple and could be accomplished by persons with relatively little training. As indicated earlier, the production of clocks by cottage industry in the region near Morbier was adapted to economic conditions that persisted for more than a century. So if the clock was so successful, why did it pass away so quickly? One factor was certainly changing tastes. The Morbier clock in its homely pine case represented a static, rural society of the nineteenth century. With the shift of population to the cities and the improvement in transportation and communication, people wanted something more modern. With smaller houses and people moving into apartments, wall clocks became popular because they didn't take up valuable floor space. In the late nineteenth and early twentieth centuries chime clocks imitating the chimes of Big Ben in London became the "in" thing. The clockmakers of the Morbier district of the Jura began to produce the models currently in demand, and the production of the Morbier clock described above began to decline in the decade of the 1890s.

With the development of railroads the dairy industry of the Jura could find more distant markets, and production for sale replaced subsistence farming, so the young people who did not move to the city found it less necessary to work on clocks in the winter to augment their income from the farm. The dislocation of World War I, when every village and hamlet felt the strain in goods and in manpower, was the last straw. When peace returned in 1918, it was a different world with automobiles and airplanes and radio, and the Morbier clock was forgotten, to be rediscovered nearly half a century later, mainly by Americans after World War II.

Figure 37. Close-up of pinwheel escapement, showing long pallet arms.

STRIKING TRAINS

This section describes in some detail the striking mechanism, featuring the unique after strike, found in most Morbier clocks. There are also general treatments of the quarter strike, alarm mechanism, and calendar, and some additional notes on the historical development of the striking train.

There is considerable variety in the striking mechanism of Morbier clocks. Most strike the hour, repeating a minute or two later (the after strike), and strike the half hour with the same mechanism. Others strike and repeat the hour, but the half hour has a passing strike using a pin on the minute wheel and a separate hammer. In the quarter strike there are two-train and three-train movements, some having the after strike and some not. A few three-train, quarter strike clocks repeat the hour with each quarter (grande sonnerie). Almost all are based on the same rugged mechanism with a snail and a double-sided rack (which the French call echelle, or ladder) that

Figure 38, above. Front quarter view of strike mechanism of late Morbier showing general arrangement of parts.

drops vertically instead of pivoting. This mechanism is also notable in that it has no delay or warning; the train is released to strike at the time the rack drops. The following paragraphs describe in some detail this basic mechanism; the variations will be described more briefly.

The Basic Mechanism

Figures 38 and 39 are overall views of the basic mechanism found in most Morbier clocks made between the French Revolution and World War I. As noted in the time train description, one can see the heavy, cut wheels and the substantial handwrought parts of the strike mechanism. The function of the various parts can be better understood with the aid of Fig-

Figure 39, left. Rear quarter view of clock in Figure 38.

ure 40, a schematic diagram of the essential parts of the mechanism. Some liberties have been taken with details for purposes of clarity, but it should be possible to identify the corresponding features in the photographs or in a clock if you have one at hand.

In the diagram, D (Figure 40) is a detent that arrests the striking train when stop pin Q, which is mounted in the rim of the third wheel of the striking train, comes to rest on notch Z. In the diagram this is shown on the front face of the wheel, but in most instances the pin, detent, etc. are on the rear face (Figure 41). The detent is fast on shaft L, which also carries pawl S, which in turn operates on rack F. The latter has teeth on both sides and slides vertically, held in alignment by two rods T and T', which are carried in guides riveted to the main support bar.

M is the minute hand arbor that carries cam I, which actuates the strike mechanism once on the half hour and twice on the hour in the manner peculiar to Morbier clocks (to be described later). Strike release A has a forked end that rides on cam I (Figure 42a). This lever is fastened to arbor K, which carries bent lever B pivoted to trip piece C. The latter engages projection P of detent D either at the end or in a notch on the lower side (Figures 43 and 44). Earlier models have two notches on the lower side and a curlicue at the end as shown in the diagram and in Figures 45 and 46 (see page 30), but they function in the same manner.

The operation of the mechanism is as follows: When the first point of the fork on strike release lever A drops off cam I, the lever assumes the position shown in Figure 42b, being retained in an intermediate position by the second point resting on the cam. In so doing, it actuates trip C, the first notch (or the end) of which rests against projection P (Figure 43). In thrusting to the left (diagram) or to the right (Figure 43), it pushes detent D free of pin Q, releasing the train, and because pawl S is also fastened to the same arbor, the rack falls. The number of teeth through which the rack falls is determined by stiff wire W, which, operating in a guide, drops on snail H attached rigidly to the hour hand pipe.

As the train runs, extension G of one leaf of the pinion on the third wheel arbor (Figure 47, see page 30) lifts the rack one tooth for each blow struck and pawl S retains the tooth gained. As long as the pawl engages the teeth of the rack, it holds detent D clear of pin Q and the train continues to run. When the rack is fully raised, the pawl drops into the last notch N. This notch is deeper than the others or else the rack is undercut after the last tooth as in Figure 47. This causes notch Z of detent D to engage pin Q and arrest the train.

At this time, the notch of trip C (or the second notch of earlier models) is resting against projection P (Figure 44) since lever A is in the intermediate position as shown in Figure 42b. When cam I moves about 12° (in approximately two minutes), the second point Y of the fork drops off the cam, lever A moves to the position shown in Figure 42c, and trip C again releases the train, causing the clock to strike the hour as before.

On the half hour, strike release lever A moves a smaller distance as determined by the smaller notch in the cam or shorter break in the hoop wheel. This is enough to release pin Q but not enough to cause the rack to fall. The

Figure 40. Schematic diagram of the strike mechanism as seen from the front.

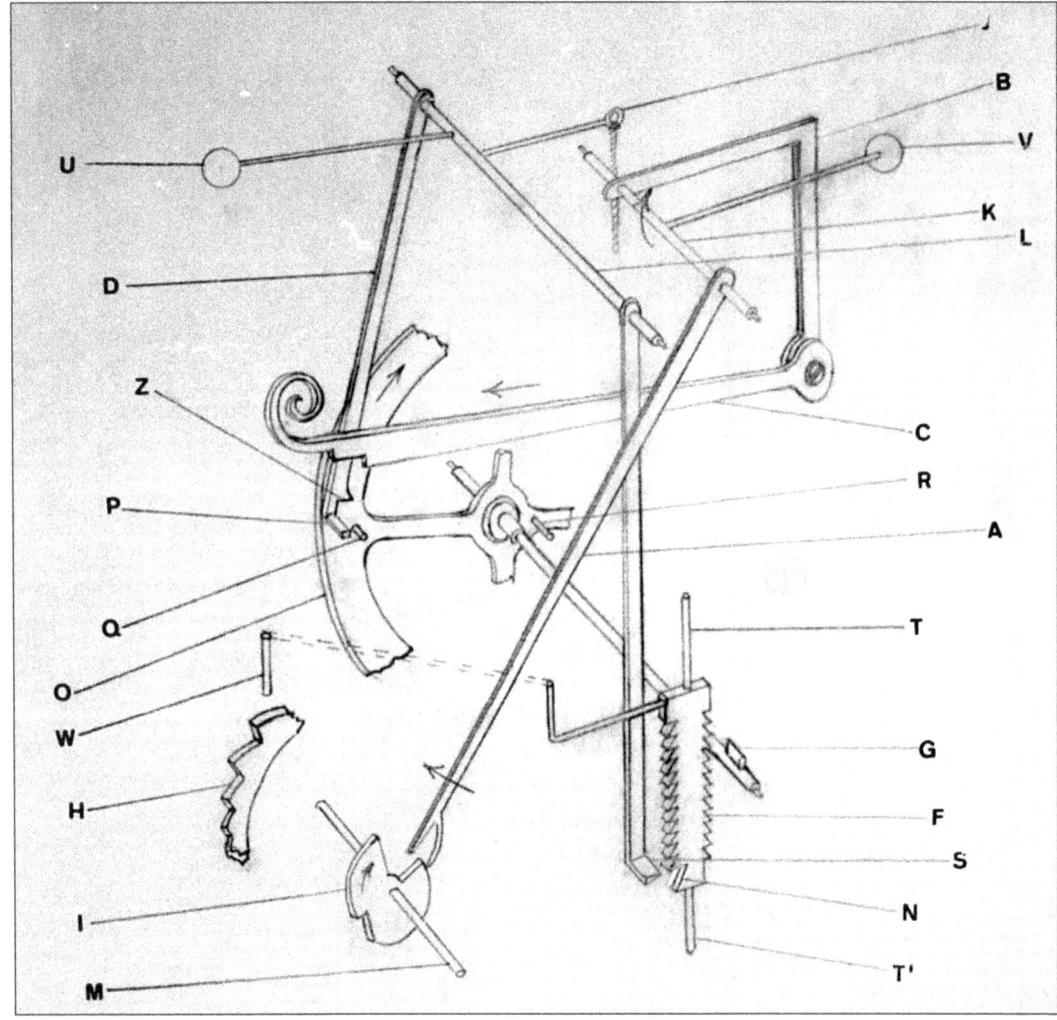

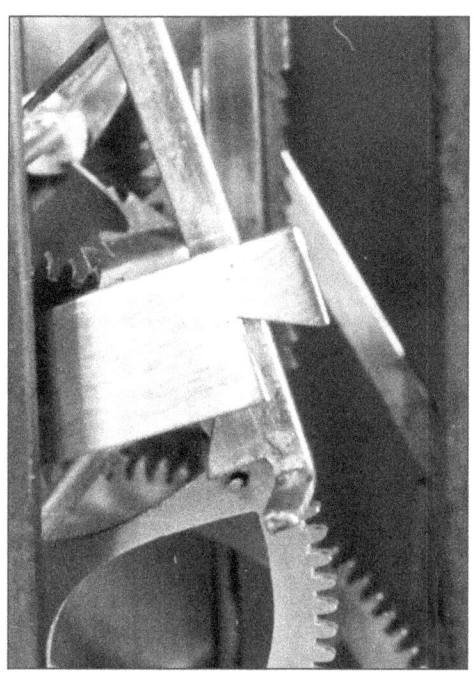

Figure 41, left. Detail of late model showing pin held by detent; trip piece is raised here but usually rests on or against projection of detent. Detail is seen from rear of clock.

Figures 42a-42c, right; top to bottom. Detail of the strike release lever and cam as seen from the rear: (a) as it is about to drop for the first strike of the hour; (b) after first release; and (c) after second release. Note that cam I of the schematic diagram is in the form of a hoop wheel in this example.

Figure 43, left. Trip piece resting against detent before striking begins as seen from rear of clock.

third wheel makes one revolution allowing one blow to be struck before pin Q is arrested by Z. In some clocks there is no second notch in the cam, and the half hour is struck with a separate hammer operated by a lever, which is lifted and released by a pin on the minute wheel. Some details of this mechanism are described in the following paragraph.

Two other points should be mentioned. First, there is pin R, mounted near the arbor of the second wheel, which is so arranged that it lifts trip C once each revolution at the proper time so that detent D is free to move to the right (diagram) and engage pin Q. Second, as cam I revolves further, after the hour has struck the second time, it pushes back the strike release lever to its original position, which in turn causes trip C to slide to the right (diagram) across projection P so that it finally ends up in the original position shown in Figure 43.

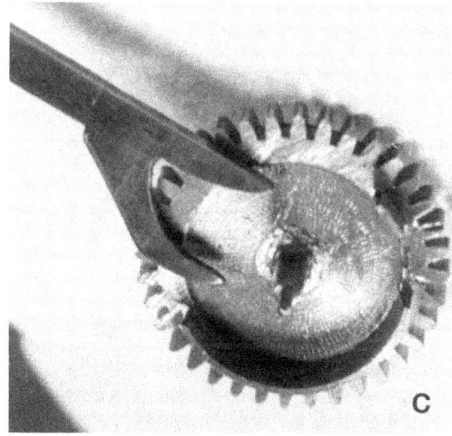

Figure 44, left. Detent resting in notch after first strike.
Figure 45, right. Earlier model detent with two notches and remnant of curlicue.

In the later models (Figures 38 and 39; see page 27) there are no springs in the strike mechanism. Instead, there are two counterweights: U, which acts on arbor L controlling the pawl, and V, which acts to press strike release lever A against the cam or hoop wheel. It should be noted that in the earlier models (Figure 46) the curlicue served a useful purpose, that is, as additional weight to ensure that the trip piece dropped promptly to engage the projection of the detent. In later models, one finds the trip piece is made heavier, thus accomplishing the same purpose without having the extra work of making the curlicue.

This strike mechanism also functions as a repeater. On most clocks you will find lever J on the detent arbor to which a cord is attached. This cord may be pulled at any time regardless of the state of the mechanism and the hour will be struck. Inasmuch as the snail is mounted directly on the hour wheel pipe and not actuated by a star wheel, the clock will strike the following hour for some time before the hour actually arrives.

From the repairer's standpoint this mechanism has another useful feature. All the critical timing factors are established at the time of manufacture of the third wheel and its arbor. In reassembling the movement one has only to check the relation of the third to the second wheel, which has either notches or pins to lift the hammer, to ensure that the hammer is not partially lifted when the train is arrested; for if it is, the train may not start when released due to the extra friction. Figure 48 ahead shows a detailed view of the lower end of the hammer arbor, which in most Morbiers is rotated about the vertical axis by a notched wheel rather than by pins. In this view you can also notice a replacement hammer spring that is too long for this movement.

The end of this spring is turned to a smaller diameter so that the shoulder thus created will prevent the hammer arbor from rising out of the lower cock. In this clock it was necessary to turn a new shoulder on the spring at the proper length before the strike would operate properly.

Figure 49 shows a detail of the strike release lever arbor of an earlier model clock that has a flat spring and roller to ensure that the lever always presses against the cam. Note also that this arbor is pivoted in the fixed posts of the cage, retained by a dovetailed key, and not in the bars that carry the other moving parts. In the background you may also be able to see another flat spring riveted into the upright bar, which acts on the detent arbor in place of the other counterweight. Figure 50 shows the rack of this clock, which is of steel instead of brass. The guide rods top and bottom and the control rod that drops on the snail are all forged in one piece, and the teeth are hand-filed. In Figures 49 and 51 (see page 32) note the fairly high steeple and the fanciful shape of the bell hammer, which indicate this is a clock of the bronze-front period.

Figure 46. Trip piece with curlicue counterweight of earlier model Morbier probably dating from the time of the French Revolution (1789-1793).

Figure 47, right. The "ladder" rack and lifting pawl, which is one leaf of the pinion left long.

Figure 48, above left. Detail of hammer arbor and hammer spring (which in this case did not fit the movement).

Figure 49, above right. Detail of strike release lever arbor with flat spring instead of counterweight. Note dovetail key, which holds arbor in place at upper right, and two-leaf fly.

Figure 50, left. Forged one-piece steel rack guides and control rod of earlier model clock.

Figure 51. Passing strike mechanism as found in two-hand Morbier of late eighteenth century.

Figure 52. Heavy iron fly of early Morbier.

Figure 51 shows the passing strike also found on this clock. Although differing somewhat in detail, it functions exactly as the half hour strike on the clock of the early period illustrated in Figure 41 (see page 29). It is obvious that there are more parts in this independent half hour strike than in the type in which it is combined with the hour strike. It may be that some time elapsed between the development of the repeating strike characteristic of Morbier clocks and the adaptation to also strike the half hours, which would be cheaper to make. It is also possible that this is an example of individuality of design on the part of the artisans making these clocks. Another possibility is that the half hour was struck on a different bell nested on the same bell stand.

Most Morbiers dating from the period of the Revolution or later have a four-leaf fly of thin brass with the usual friction spring to avoid undue shock in arresting the train. In earlier models there is some variety. Figure 52 shows a heavy iron fly found on a very early Morbier. Figure 49 (see page 31) shows a fly with only two leaves. This latter clock probably dates from 1740 to 1760.

The Gong Strike

One feature that distinguishes later model Morbiers is the gong strike. Presumably, the loud, clear bell was too powerful for the ordinary household, so they adopted a wire gong that was less obtrusive. Figure 53 shows the mechanism required little change to have the strike train ratchet act on an arbor parallel to the other arbors and actuate a small hammer, which was usually cushioned with leather. To get the necessary resonance, a wooden sounding board was fitted to the back of the frame instead of the usual black sheet iron. In the photograph notice the date April 1903 written in pencil on this sounding board. This was probably the date the clock was sold and put in service.

Figure 53. Detail of gong strike showing hammer with leather insert and sounding board that has been removed and placed alongside the clock. Note pencil date: Avril (April) 1903.

Figure 54. Rearview of Morez movement showing large spring barrels and black iron cage with steel mounting bars as in traditional Morbier clocks.

The Morez Striking Mechanism

In the earlier section on the history of the Morbier clock it was noted that the final development was a spring-driven wall clock with either the round *oeil de boeuf* (or bull's eye) case or the more ornate picture frame case decorated in mother-of-pearl inlay. The strike mechanism of the so-called Morez clock bears considerable resemblance to the later models of the traditional Morbier. However, in Figure 54 the arbor of the leather-faced hammer has been mounted in the frame itself rather than being carried on an extra bracket and the movement is much more compact, measuring only 16 centimeters (6-1/4 inches) wide by 17 centimeters (6-5/8 inches) high. To compensate for the fewer turns available from the spring-driven going barrel, compared with the weight-driven barrel, the wheel count has been modified and the strike ratchet has 28 teeth.

Figure 55. Detail of Morez picture frame clock strike mechanism showing large, heavy strike release lever in the form of an inverted U pivoted at upper left corner. The wire guide is of stamped brass and the trip piece of pressed steel with some evidence of hand finishing.

A separate counterweight is retained to press the gathering pawl against the rack, but Figure 55 shows the strike release lever acts as its own counterweight, being bent into a U-shape and pivoted in the center bar at the upper left. The ladder-type rack is moved to the front of the upright bar, and there is a double lifting pawl made of brass, so that two blows are struck for each revolution of the third wheel, which has two stop pins instead of one as in the traditional Morbier. The hour is repeated two minutes later and the construction, although more compact, resembles the earlier weight-driven clocks except that a few parts are made of stamped or pressed brass and mild steel, in contrast to the cut brass and wrought iron parts used in weight-driven clocks right up to the end of production.

Quarter Strike Mechanisms

There are two basic types of quarter strike mechanisms: (1) those with separate trains for striking the quarters and the hours as in most chiming clocks and (2) those with only one striking train. Unlike the ting-tang quarter strike found in other clocks of European origin, which have an elaborate count wheel to strike both the quarters and the hours, most Morbiers have two snails that control the single ladder rack.

Figure 56. Rearview of two-train, three-bell, quarter-striking Morbier showing general arrangement.

They also have a shifting mechanism to strike the hours on a different bell from those used for the quarters. Three-train Morbiers have three or more bells, usually strike the fourth quarter before the hour, and may repeat the hour after the quarters (grande sonnerie). They may also repeat the hour (the afterstrike), but the second time without striking the fourth quarter.

From the foregoing, it may be apparent that there is a tremendous variety in Morbier clocks with quarter strike. While there were many makers, each one made relatively few clocks, so it is unusual to find two that are exactly the same. The following paragraphs describe typical examples of the two-train and the three-train types, but it must be recognized that any clock that the reader may be fortunate enough to find will vary in detail and sometimes in principle.

Two-Train, Three-Bell Quarter Strike

Figure 56 is an overall rearview of an example of this type of clock that shows the general layout of the parts. The two bells on each side strike the quarters in ting-tang fashion, one stroke on each bell for the first quarter, two on each for the second, and three on each for the third. On the hour the two quarter bells are silent, and the hour is struck on the large central bell, which is pitched somewhat lower than the other two. On this particular example the hour is repeated two minutes later as on regular Morbier clocks.

Figure 57. The two snails and the two wires that control the single rack of a two-train, three-bell Morbier.

Figure 58. Detailed view of the two snails, the hoop wheel release cam, and the roller lifting lever that shifts the mechanism to strike the hours.

Figure 57 shows the hour snail on the hour wheel pipe and the quarter snail behind it on the minute wheel arbor. Above can be seen the two wires that control the single rack of the usual Morbier-type strike mechanism. The hour snail is specially cut to strike the second and third quarters after 1 o'clock with the same rack. Figure 58 shows the snails separately; notice the notch in the 1 o'clock sector of the hour snail to provide clearance for the rack to fall so that the second and third quarters can be struck. Likewise, the 2 o'clock sector is cut short so that the third quarter can be struck after 2 o'clock. The quarter snail has only three steps and a large blank sector so that the wire can fall as far as necessary to strike the hours from 1 to 12. Also on the minute wheel arbor is the hoop wheel cam with three small openings to release the quarters and a larger opening to permit the strike release lever to drop twice on the hour to provide the afterstrike.

On the end of the minute hand arbor can be seen (Figure 58) the small lever with a roller that shifts the hammer mechanism so that the hours are struck on the large bell and the quarters on the smaller bells as described in the next paragraphs.

Figure 59 shows a detailed view of the shift mechanism

Figure 59, left. Detail of the shift mechanism as seen from the rear of the clock.

that is fitted at the back of the clock. To the right is the roller on the end of the minute wheel arbor, which lifts the bell crank and shifts the horizontal arbor to the right in the photograph. This disengages the two pallets that otherwise strike the two quarter bells in ting-tang fashion and engage another pallet that operates the hour-bell hammer. In the photograph the roller is shown in the position about five minutes after the hour has struck. In another ten minutes, it will have become completely free of the bell crank, and the mechanism will again be in a position to strike the quarters.

This clever design provides a quarter strike with relatively few additional parts. Like the basic Morbier strike, it cannot get out of step with the hands, and there are no complicated timing factors in assembly. Other than the free movement of the train before hammer lift, the only critical factor is the relation of the hour hand arbor and its snail to the minute hand arbor. Proper positioning will ensure that the rack is free to drop two or three steps after 1 and 2 o'clock. The strike-train weight on Morbier quarter striking clocks with three and more bells is always heavier than those on regular clocks because two or more hammers have to be lifted at nearly the same time. In addition, the number of blows struck in 24 hours is such that the wheel count has to be higher for the same weight drop. In this example, for instance, in 24 hours there are 144 double (ting-tang) blows for the quarters and 156 single blows for the hours. The strike weight for this clock weighs 8 kilograms or nearly 18 pounds, compared with 7 or 8 pounds for the going train.

Figure 60. Front view of three-train, three-bell clock.

Three-Train, Three-Bell Striking Mechanisms

Figure 60 shows the overall appearance of this type of Morbier. The going train with verge escapement is in the center; on the right-hand side is the quarter striking train, which strikes the quarters in ting-tang fashion on the two smaller bells. On the left side is the hour train, which strikes the hours (with afterstrike) on the large bell. Unlike the two-train clock described above, it strikes four double blows at the hour before the hour is struck the first time.

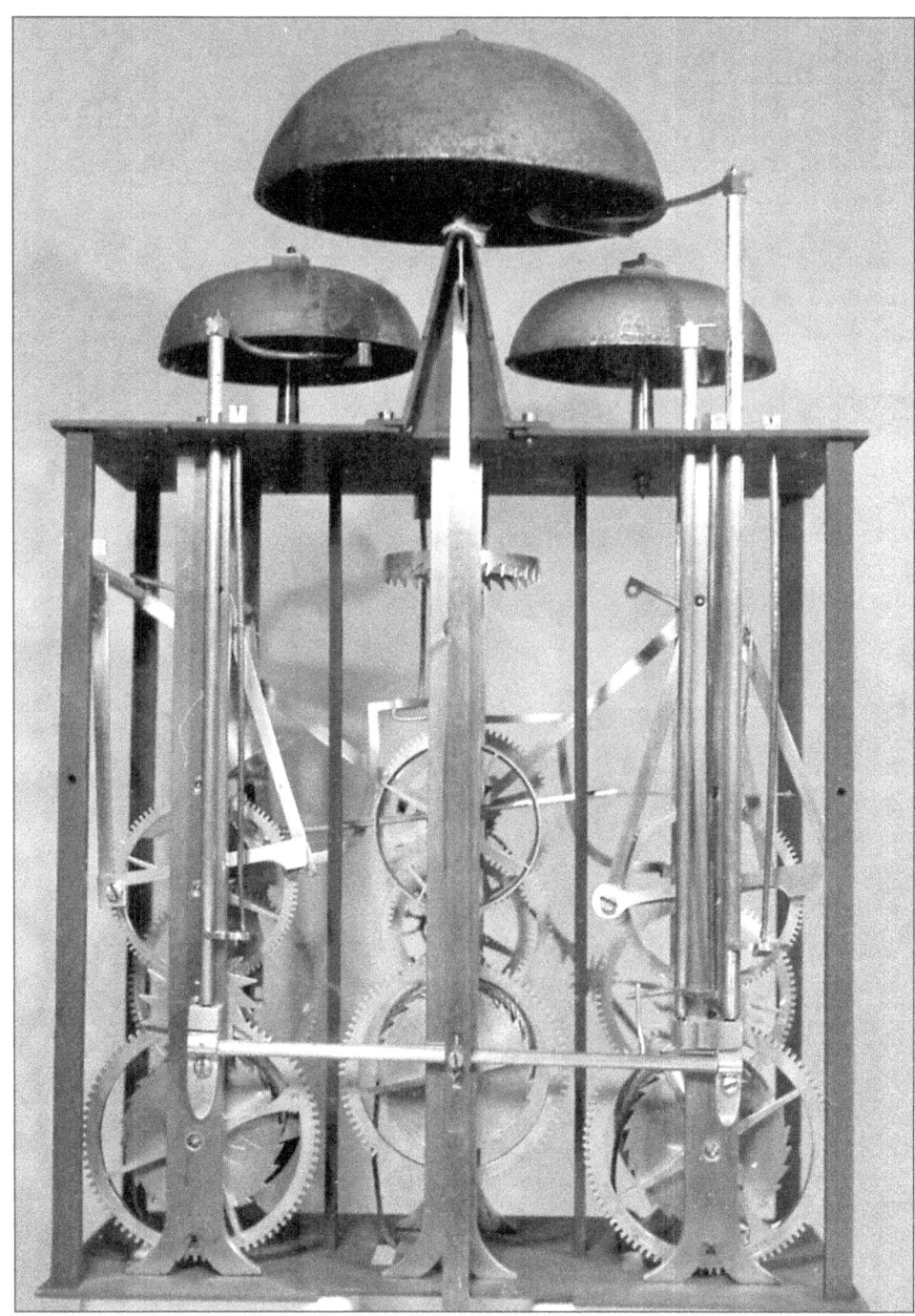

Figure 61. Rearview of three-train, quarter-striking Morbier. Note absence of shifting mechanism.

Although there are many more parts in the three-train clock, the action is much simpler because the two trains function independently. Figure 61 shows a rearview of the same clock. Here the connecting rod that actuates the second quarter strike bell appears on the opposite side of the clock.

The hour rack and the quarter rack are controlled independently by snails on the hour hand pipe and the minute hand arbor, respectively. Figure 62 is a close-up showing how the two strike release levers, which slant diagonally toward the center arbor, are positioned to be acted upon by the minute arbor cam, which in this clock is in the form of four pins. Figure 63 shows that one of these pins is longer than the other three so that it alone actuates the hour train release lever as the hour approaches. All four pins operate the quarter strike release lever, which lies in a plane closer to the minute wheel than does the hour strike release lever.

When properly adjusted, both strike release levers drop simultaneously on the hour and the quarter strike train is free to run. As the quarter rack hook is lifted to let the quarter rack drop, it thrusts a rod into the fly of the hour strike train, arresting it until the quarter train rack hook drops into the deeper notch of the quarter rack at the conclusion of the quarter strike. This last action arrests the quarter train and at the same time releases the hour train to strike the hour. In Figure 62 this rod holds one leaf of the hour train fly as the quarter

Figure 62. Close-up showing the two strike release levers and the two rods controlling the hour and quarter racks.

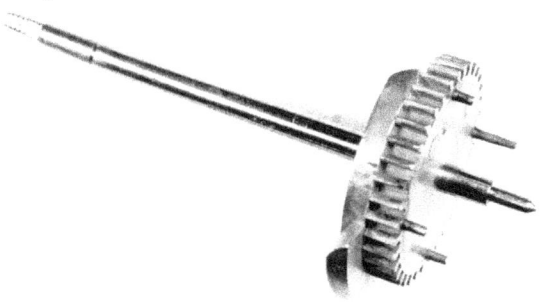

Figure 63. Detailed view of the minute wheel arbor with the quarter snail and the four pins for releasing the quarter and hour strike trains.

train rack hook is engaging one of the ordinary teeth of the quarter rack at the extreme right of the photo.

In this clock the hour train has fewer blows to strike in 24 hours than does a regular Morbier because it does not strike the half hours. Consequently, the hour train weight and the going train weight are of the usual size. The quarter train, however, strikes 240 double blows every 24 hours, and the wheel count is such that a much heavier weight is required.

As with other Morbier clocks, the strike on this type cannot get out of step with the hands even for a single quarter. There are repeater levers for both the quarter train and the hour train but on the clock shown, the loop for the cord on the quarter train side has been cut off. It probably was thought unnecessary to know the quarter when the repeater feature was used during the night.

How to Live with a Morbier

One aspect of the Morbier clock that makes it hard to live with is the loud and penetrating tone of the bell when it suddenly breaks the otherwise relative quiet of the American home. If you would like to keep one of these clocks running, something has to be done to keep your guests from looking in panic for the fire escape the first time your Morbier strikes. By changing the hammer (Figure 64), one can reduce the clamor considerably.

Since the hammer is usually soft iron, one solution is to drill a 3/16-inch-diameter hole and fit a piece of sole leather. This will mellow the tone and reduce the volume by about half. I prefer, however, to remove the hammerhead from the

Figure 64. Original iron hammerhead drilled to receive leather plug; chime clock hammer fitted to original striker arm (two ways of cutting down the clamor).

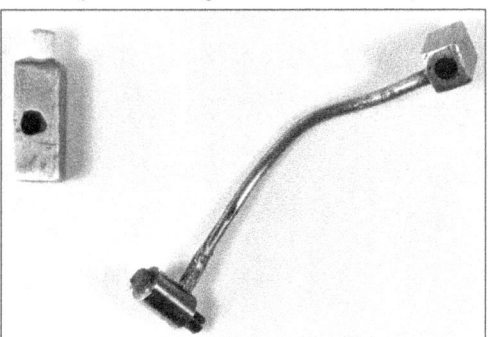

Figure 65. Alarm disc and release as found on late model Morbier.

strike arm and replace it with a lighter hammer taken from a chime clock. Because of the lighter weight of the smaller brass hammer, the volume of sound is still further reduced, and the original hammer is available, unmarred, if one wishes to restore the clock to its original condition. There is one disadvantage to reducing the volume of the bell sound, namely, that the noise of the train may become more audible. But this is a small price to pay for a little more peace and quiet.

Alarm Mechanism

Figure 65 shows the essential parts of the alarm mechanism as fitted to the majority of clocks made during the nineteenth century. A cam is friction-fitted on the hour hand pipe and can be turned to the proper hour by the alarm disc, which is located in front of the dial. To set the clock to go off at 6 o'clock, one turns this disc until the 6 is under the hour hand of the clock itself; this in turn orients the cam so that the alarm will be released when the hour hand reaches the 6 o'clock position. The detent is pivoted in the cage and has a V-shaped notch that holds a pin riveted in the hammer arbor motionless until the end of the detent drops off the cam. The motive power is a small weight and a very simple verge escapement working directly on the hammer arbor (Figure 66). The hammer is T-shaped, and because both ends strike the large bell on a typical Morbier clock, enough din is made to wake the soundest sleeper. There is no shutoff; it rings until it runs down—only a few seconds.

Figure 66. Friction-driven drum and simple verge escapement of alarm mechanism.

Figure 67. Working gears of simple calendar mechanism commonly found on clocks of the later period.

Calendar Mechanism

Another feature frequently found on the nineteenth-century brass front clocks is a simple calendar mechanism. An extra wheel on the hour-hand pipe turns an idler wheel once in 24 hours. Midway on one of the crossings is fixed a pin that turns the 31-tooth calendar star wheel one tooth at midnight. A spring-mounted roller maintains the star wheel in position until the next move. Figure 67 shows this is simply a wire riveted into the left-hand front post of the cage. The calendar hand is usually about one-half the length of the minute hand and is mounted on a pipe that turns loosely on the hour-hand pipe. These details and photos are given to assist those who may wish to replace broken or missing parts on clocks they have acquired.

In addition to these simple calendar mechanisms, elaborate perpetual calendar mechanisms also showed the month, day of the month, day of the week, and phases of the moon, but these are seldom found today.

Historical Notes

One of the fascinating aspects of collecting clocks is to try to trace their historical development by studying certain characteristics of the mechanisms. In the 200 years during which Morbier or Comtoise clocks were made, the makers tried many different solutions to the various problems presented, and the strike mechanism is a particularly fertile field for study. The following comments on the relative ages of various clocks are based on my observations of clocks I have owned or examined.

Figure 68 shows from left to right two single-hand clocks dating probably from the early eighteenth century and one of the mid-eighteenth century with two hands that still has the passing strike. The one on the left has an anchor escapement that is unusual, but the relatively small cage (18.5 centimeters [7-1/4 inches] high by 21.5 centimeters [8-1/2 inches] wide), the absence of "feet" on the support posts, and the evidence of handwork place it quite early in the series. This is also the clock mentioned in the earlier sections that has the circular rack with teeth on both sides like the "ladder" rack on the later Morbier clocks. The center clock has a very high steeple for the thread suspension at the rear; the cage is about the same size, and the supports have the beginnings of "feet." Close inspection reveals that the verge is above the escape wheel as in lantern clocks, which also indicates it is an early eighteenth-century model.

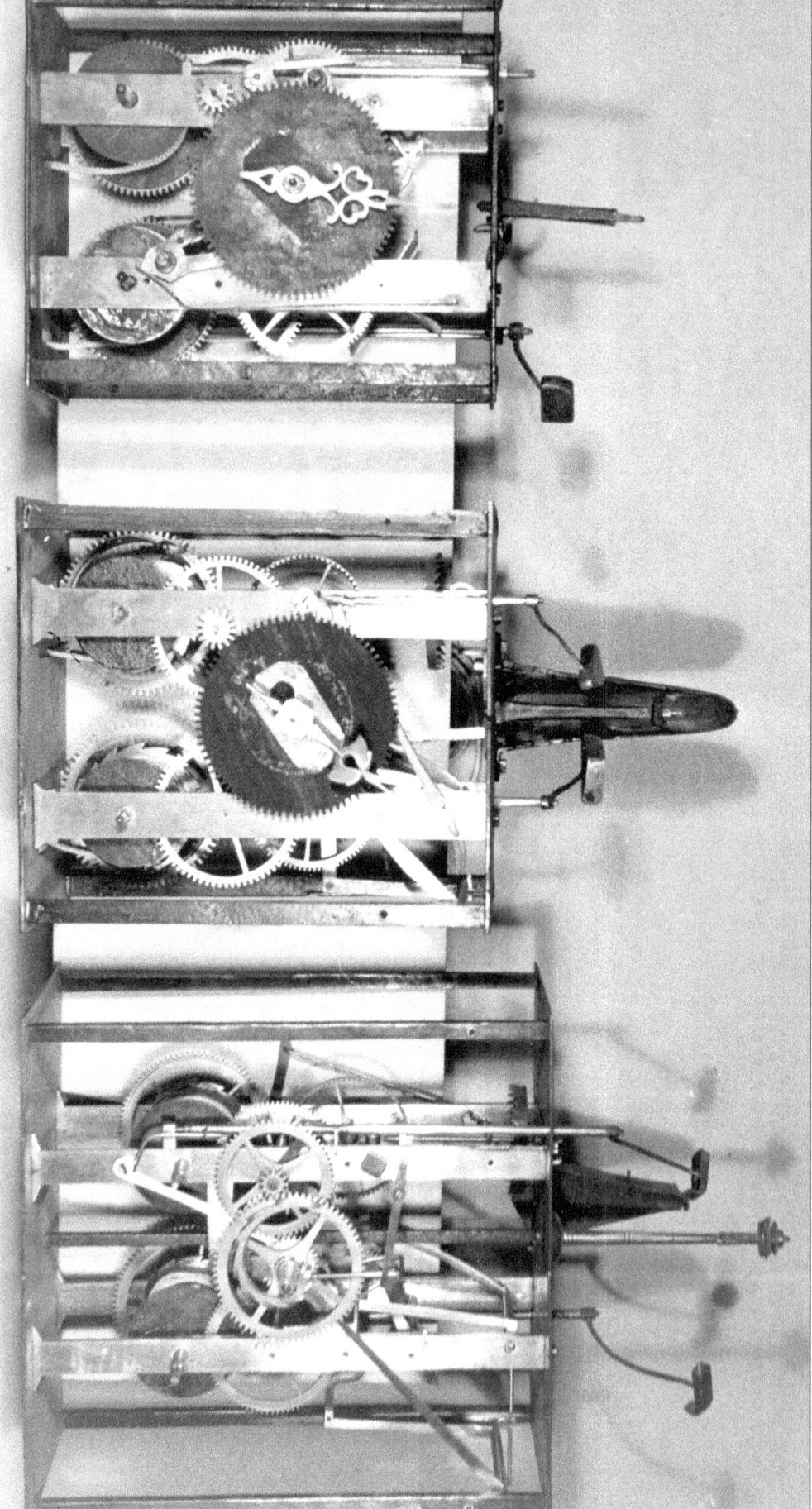

Figure 68. Three early Morbier clocks dating from the eighteenth century.

Figure 69. Detail of strike mechanism of one-hand clock dating from first half of the eighteenth century (hour wheel removed and reserved to show snail and 12-point star wheel).

Figure 68 (left) shows a later eighteenth-century clock that has a larger cage (25 centimeters [9-3/4 inches] high by 24 centimeters [9-1/2 inches] wide), almost the same size as the standard for most of the nineteenth century (25 centimeters [9-3/4 inches] by 25 centimeters). All three clocks have springs rather than counterweights in the strike mechanism, and the cord barrels are of wood with sheet iron flanges, one of which can be released by a quarter turn so that the cord can be replaced without dismantling the clock.

Figure 69 is a close-up of the passing strike and the hour wheel of the center clock in Figure 68. The hour wheel is driven by the one-hand lantern clock and carries the snail and the 12-tooth star wheel, which releases the strike train every hour. The star wheel also actuates the passing strike lever in the upper left center of the photograph. Handwork is evident in the filing of the crossings of the wheels and in the shaping of the moving parts of the strike mechanism.

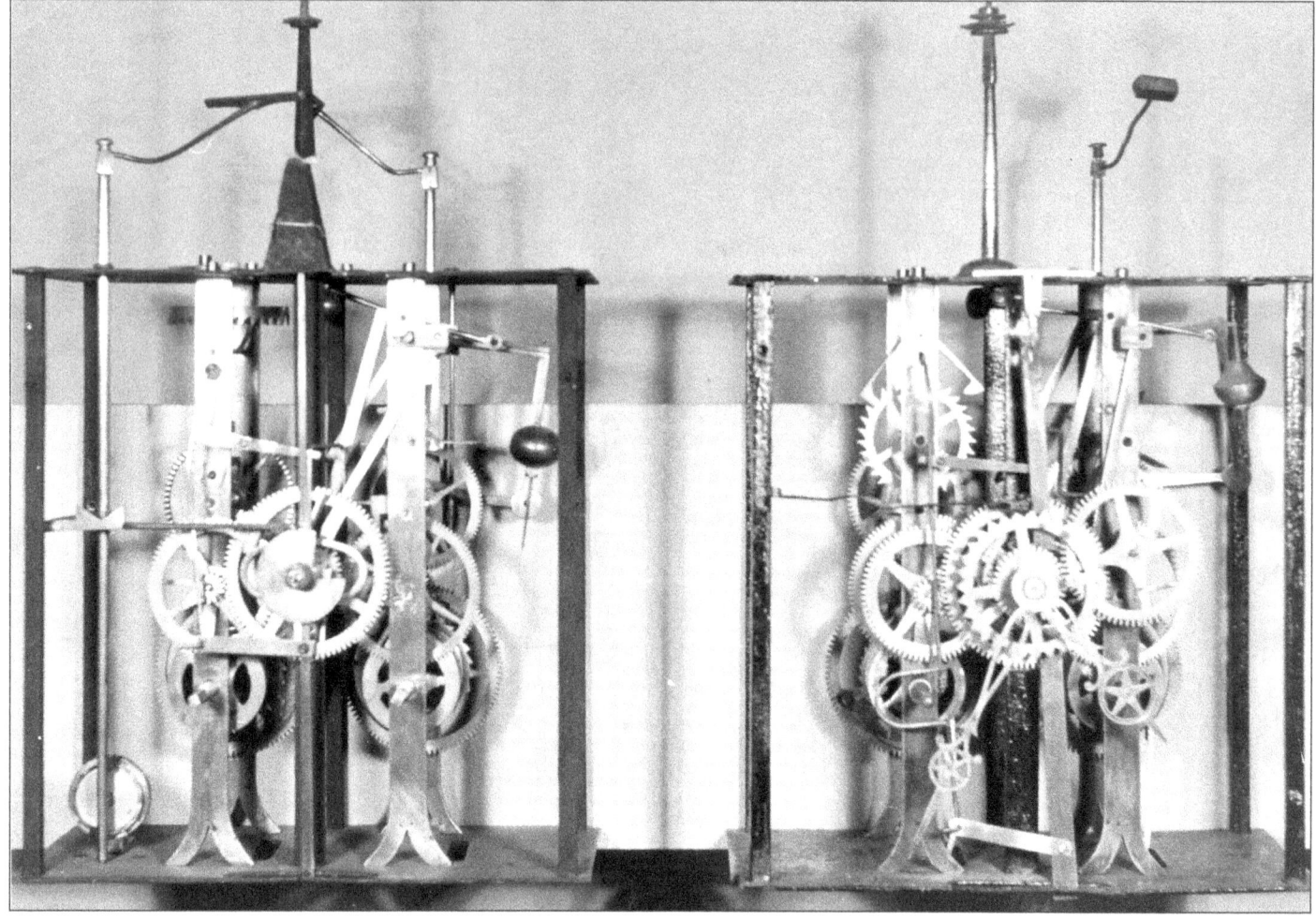

Figure 70. Mid-nineteenth-century verge escapement clock (left); late nineteenth-century anchor escapement model (right).

The clock on the left in Figure 70 is an example of a mid-nineteenth-century clock of the early brass front period described in the chronological chart (on page 12). This example has an alarm mechanism, verge escapement, and the split-foot column, standard characteristics of the later Morbiers. The pendulum is at the front but still has a thread suspension in the relatively low "steeple." On the right is a late nineteenth-century clock with anchor escapement and suspension spring for the front-mounted pendulum. Both clocks have counterweights rather than springs in the strike mechanism, and the cord barrels are of brass. These are the clocks that are most commonly found because they were produced by the tens of thousands in the mountains of the Jura and shipped all over France and nearby Switzerland and Germany.

Morbier clocks have been made in the Franche Comte in the form of kits. They were also available assembled for wall mounting or in handsome hardwood or pine cases decorated in the traditional fashion. The anchor movements are made in the authentic manner with black iron cage, heavy cut wheels and pinions turning in brass bushings mounted in polished steel support bars just as they were being made when changing tastes and social upheaval led to their demise at the beginning of World War I. But tastes have changed again and the nostalgia for the honest virtues of a simpler life has brought them back on the market again.

RESTORATION AND REPAIR

In this section principal attention will be devoted to the disassembly, cleaning, reassembly, and adjustment of the classic Morbier with verge escapement. There are also brief references to the anchor escapement and tips on restoration and the minor repairs most frequently needed. The general principles contained in this section will also apply to the more complicated quarter-striking clocks, but the variety is so great among them that it is not practical to treat them in detail. The striking mechanism of the Morez clocks of the picture frame type is also similar, although substantial changes were made in the design to make it more compact. Much of the information contained in this section will nevertheless be applicable to the restoration of those clocks as well.

For terms and additional details on the position, shape, and functioning of the various parts, refer to earlier sections. The terms differ somewhat from the literal translation of the French terms, but they are consistent with English and American usage. Figure 71 gives the names of the principal parts of the strike mechanism; the terms used for the going train should be self-explanatory.

Figure 71. Principal parts in the Morbier strike mechanism.

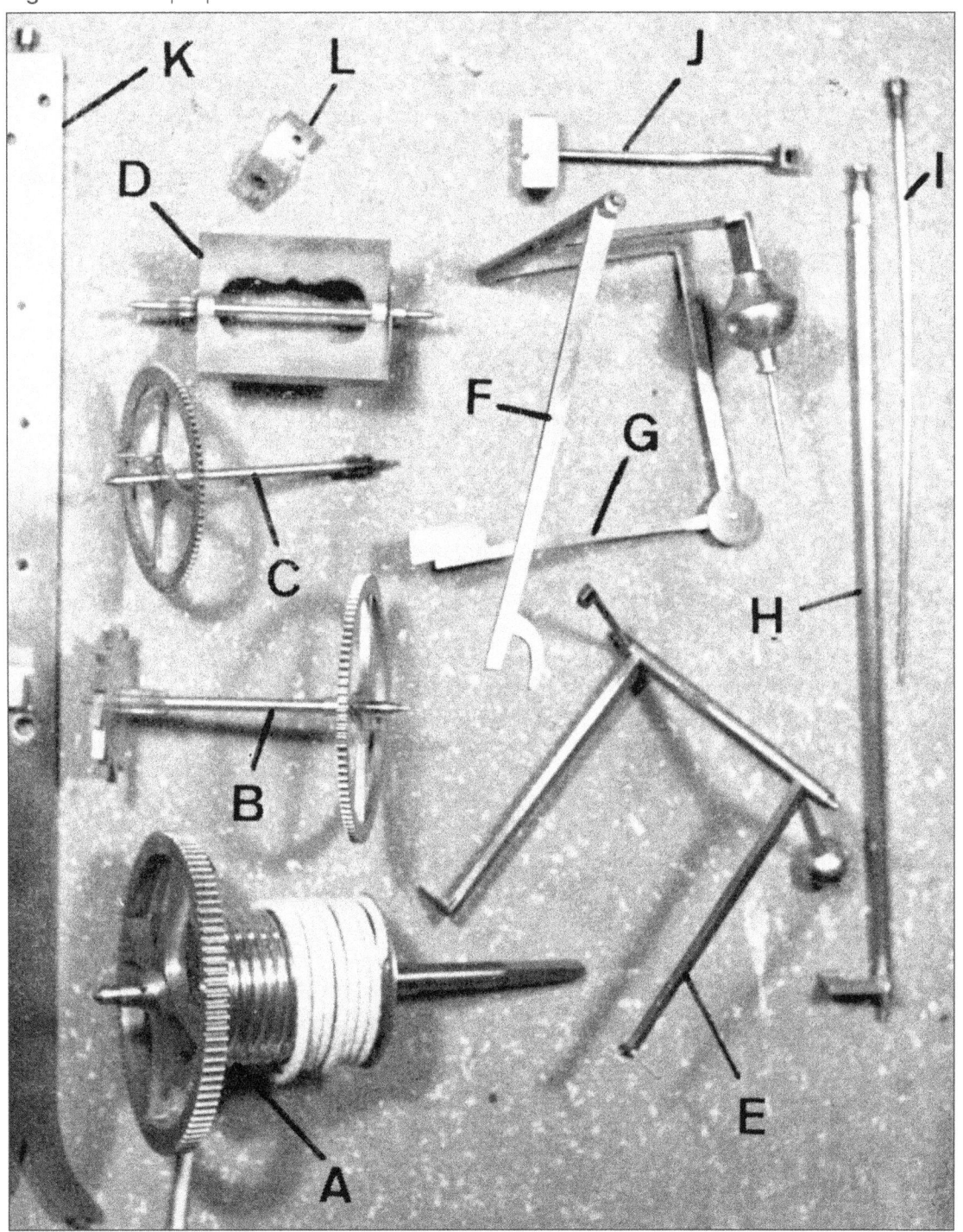

A. Barrel
B. Strike Wheel with Ratchet
C. Stop Wheel
D. Fly
E. Detent
F. Strike Release
G. Trip Piece
H. Hammer Arbor
I. Hammer Spring
J. Hammer
K. Rear Mounting Post (strike side)
L. Strike Release Cock

The construction of a Morbier clock makes it relatively easy to work on. The rugged parts, heavy wheels and pinions, generous pivots, and posted frame design are all factors that make it a good clock for a beginner. Nevertheless, there are certain critical points that should be observed to avoid damage and to ensure that the clock will continue to function properly.

Because of its simple construction, only a few ordinary tools are needed. A medium-sized screwdriver with 3/16-inch bit and a pair of flat nose pliers will suffice for disassembly and reassembly. If repairs are necessary, drills and broaches, files, a small vise, and light hammer will be needed. For cleaning the wheels and pinions, regular clock-cleaning fluid is recommended with kerosene, emery cloth, or steel wool for rusted steelwork. Mineral spirits for rinsing, chalk and brushes for finishing parts, and cloths for wiping and holding parts complete the inventory.

The usual order of work in restoring clocks is to check for wear and broken parts before and during disassembly and make necessary repairs; then clean, polish, and reassemble. However, because of the very poor condition in which one finds many Morbier clocks, it is not always possible to check for wear until after the hardened oil, kitchen grease, and other dirt and grime have been removed and the parts can move freely. It is more practical, therefore, to disassemble and carry through a first cleaning and then reassemble to check for wear and proper functioning. After necessary repairs and adjustments have been completed, the final cleaning and polishing can be done with some assurance that upon final assembly no major work will have to be done.

Disassembly

Because Morbier clocks were not built to standards, many times similar parts really fit in only one place; therefore, it is important in disassembly to mark parts that go together and especially to replace screws in their respective holes as soon as possible. This will save a great deal of time in reassembly and will ensure that parts are properly aligned and the clock will function as it should. This point cannot be emphasized too strongly.

Furthermore, the following instructions apply to the great majority of nineteenth- and early twentieth-century clocks, but there are many variations in individual models. Particularly in disassembly, the clock in your hands should be studied carefully to make sure that the general instructions apply. Some exceptions and variations have been noted, but there are many more, so work slowly, and if you have an oddball, make notes or sketches to assist you in reassembly.

Begin by unscrewing the bell nut, taking care not to lose the leather washers that are usually found above and below the bell. Remove the bell and examine the bell stand. If it is badly rusted, you may want to remove it from the cage to get rid of the rust. It has a square near the bottom and is usually threaded into the top plate of the cage. There is a collar of brass that you also might want to remove and polish.

Lay the clock flat on its back, unscrew the nut on the minute hand arbor, and take off the hand washer and the minute hand. Turn the square holding the hour hand in either direction and it will come loose, freeing the hour hand (Figure 72). Remove the hour hand and then the calendar hand or alarm ring if the clock has a calendar mechanism or alarm. Replace the nut on the minute hand arbor.

You will find two screws at the upper corners of the dial surround that fasten the dial to the cage. Remove these and the dial surround will slip out of the two slots at the bottom corners. Replace the screws in their respective holes.

Figure 72. Use flat nose pliers to turn the hour hand square 1/8 turn and remove, freeing the hour hand.

Figure 73. Spring the side doors slightly to free one pin and remove.

The side doors can be sprung gently to free them from the top or bottom pivot and can thus be removed (Figure 73). The backplate is fastened with two screws and a bent-up lug at the bottom and is removed the same way as the dial. It is good to mark these parts so they can be replaced in exactly the same relative position when reassembling the clock.

With the dial off, you can see the motion work. If there is an alarm or calendar, remove the alarm snail, or the calendar star wheel and the calendar idler wheel. It is a good idea to mark the idler wheel, the hour wheel, and the intermediate wheel before disassembly to save time in reassembling, although this is an easy adjustment to make. At this point it is a good idea to brush out the dust, cobwebs, dead flies, and other accumulated debris with an old paint brush so you can see the parts better.

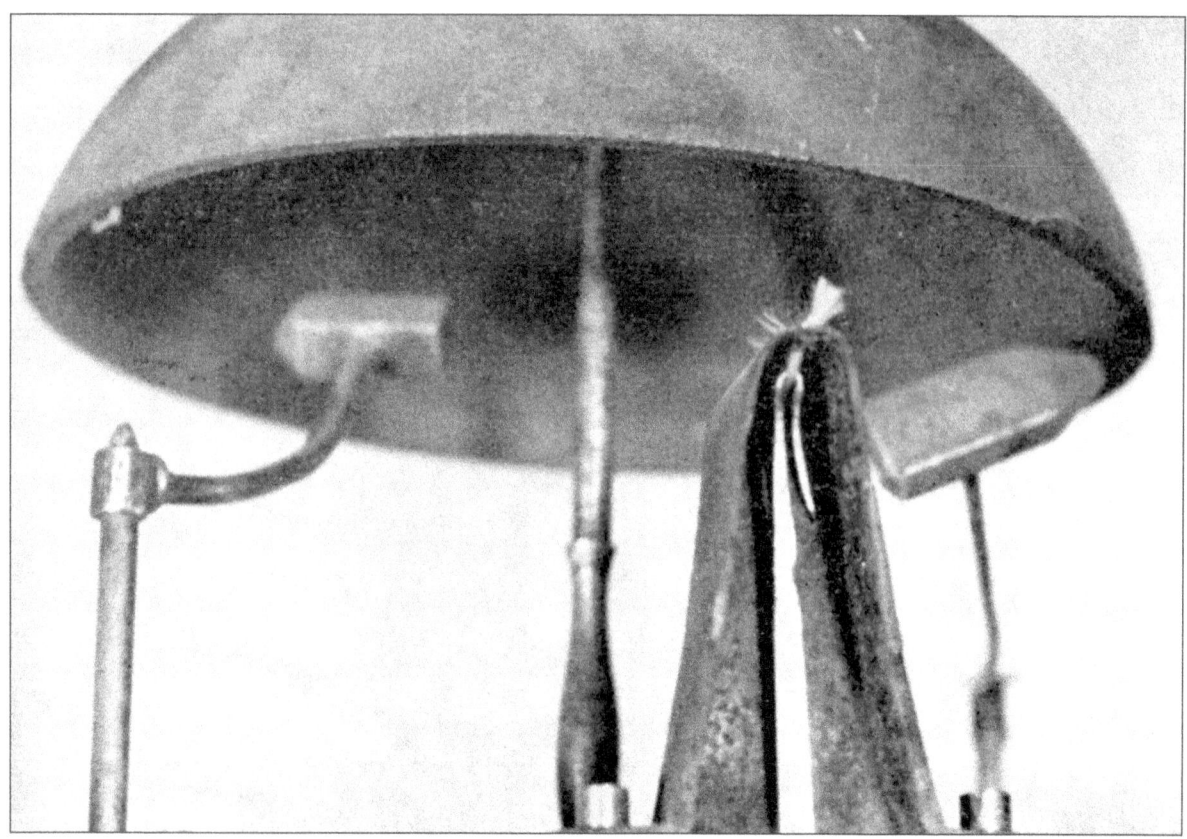

Figure 74. The "steeple" and string suspension of an early nineteenth-century Morbier verge escapement; note position at left of second hammer of independent half-hour strike.

In all but the oldest clocks the pendulum is at the front of the mechanism, and an oval stirrup of the pendulum rod surrounds the center arbor. At the top there will be either a small steeple (Figure 74) with a string suspension or a flat suspension spring (Figures 75 and 76) with a triangular hole to avoid strain on the spring when the clock is rested on a flat surface. Cut the string or

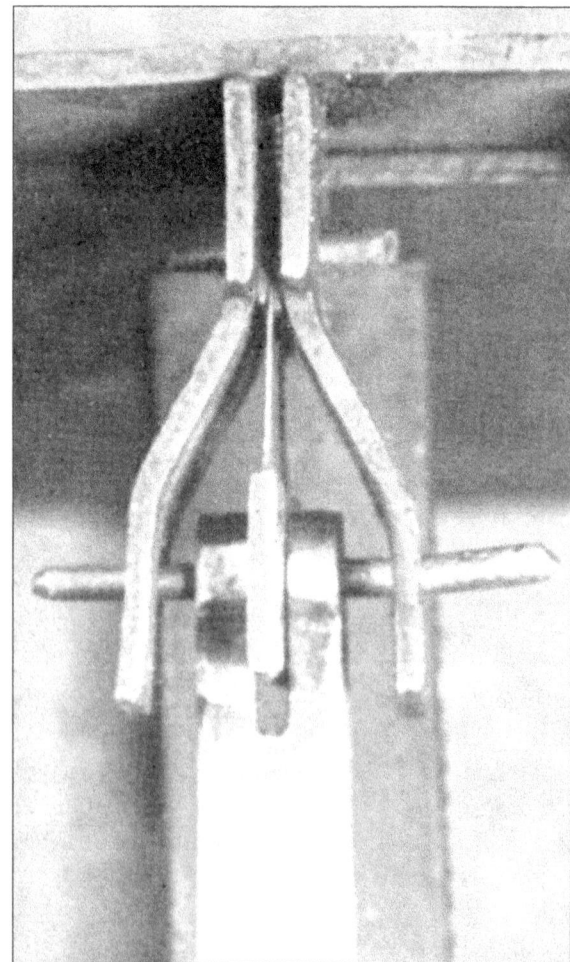 

Figures 75 and 76, right and far right. Two types of spring suspensions of late nineteenth-century Morbier with anchor escapement.

Figure 77. Removing the screw fastening the link to the pendulum rod.

unpin the spring to release the pendulum rod. This pendulum rod is linked to the verge by a flat brass strip, which is fastened by a screw with a shoulder (Figure 77).

Remove this screw, take off the link, and replace the screw. In most clocks the link can then be unhooked from the verge rod, but there are variations (Figures 78 and 79). The pendulum rod and the hour wheel can then be removed. You should examine the pendulum rod to see if it is bent. If it is, leave it that way because it was probably bent intentionally to avoid interference with the dial, the cage, the hour wheel, or other parts.

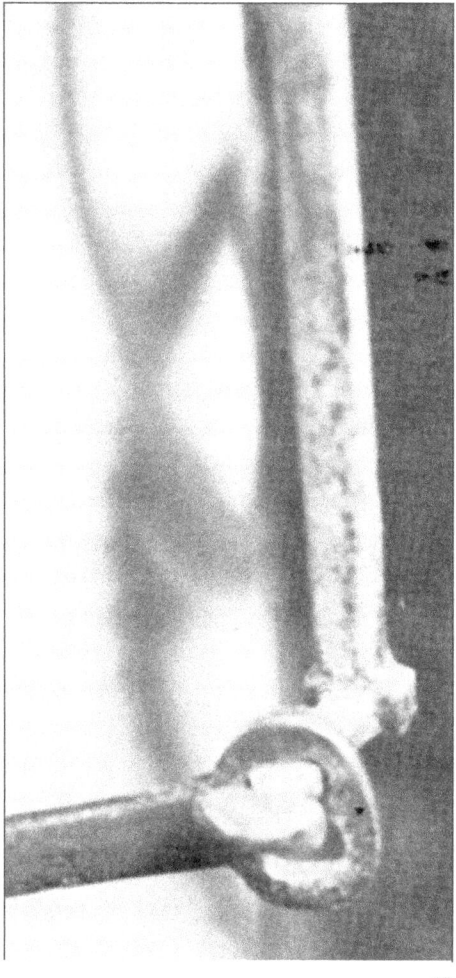

Figure 78, right. A variation in the manner of securing the link to the verge rod.

Figure 79, far right. Another variation in the linkage between the pendulum rod and the verge rod. Found on older clocks with pendulum at the rear.

Figure 80. Removing the pin from the second wheel arbor.

Figure 81. Removing the friction drive spring with two screwdrivers.

Remove the intermediate wheel, which is fixed on the second wheel arbor of the time train with a pin and a friction drive spring (Figure 80). Remove the friction spring. This is a press fit on the arbor and must be pried loose with care, to avoid bending the arbor (Figure 81). Remove the cannon wheel cock and the cannon wheel; do not forget to replace the screw.

Examine the strike hammer assembly (Figure 82) and note the relation of the strike hammer spring and the shoulder or lug, which functions to keep the hammer arbor from rising out of its cock, so you will know how to put it back together. To remove the strike hammer, first loosen the brass nut two turns, and if the hammer is not loose, support it with flat nose pliers and tap gently on the nut to free it (Figure 83). Then remove the hammer arbor and the spring that is threaded in the top plate.

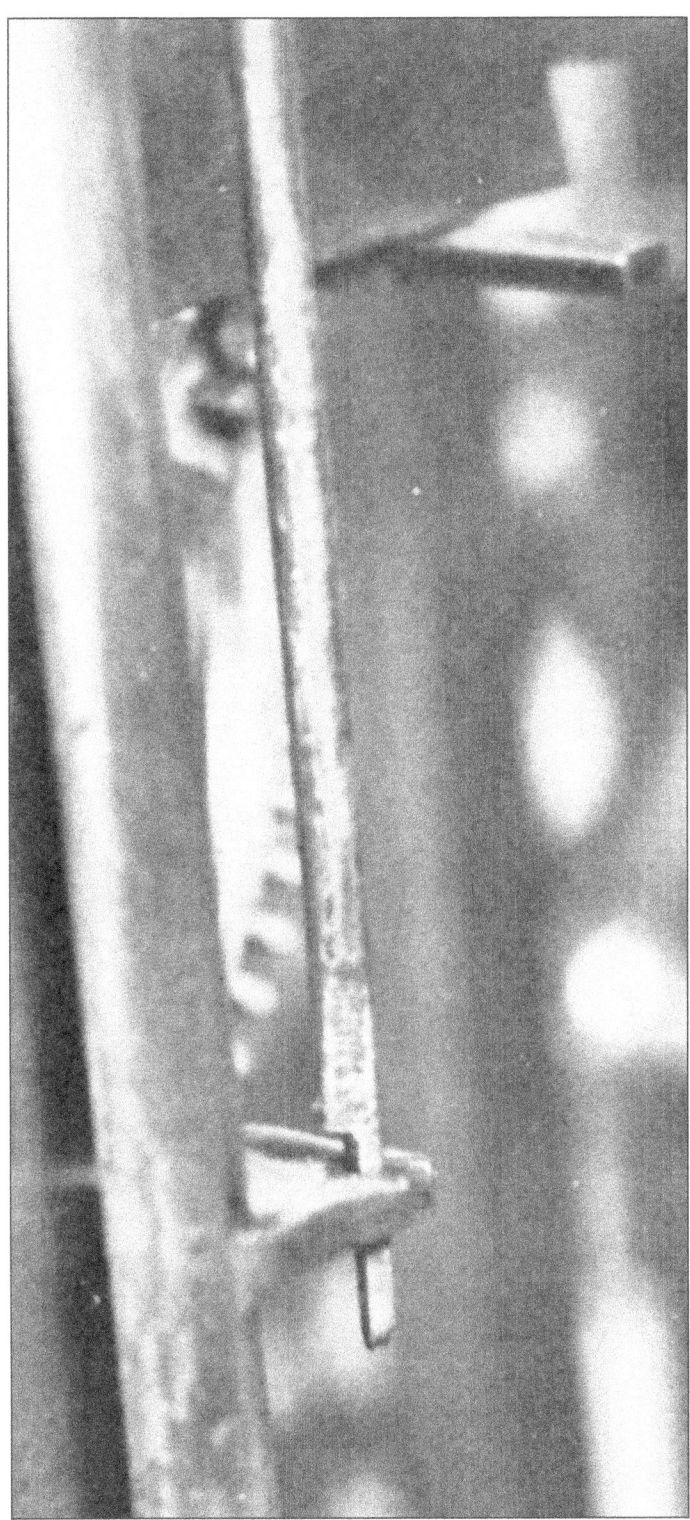

Figure 82. Detail of the hammer spring showing shoulder that keeps hammer arbor in place. When reassembling, the hammer spring should be turned to the same position.

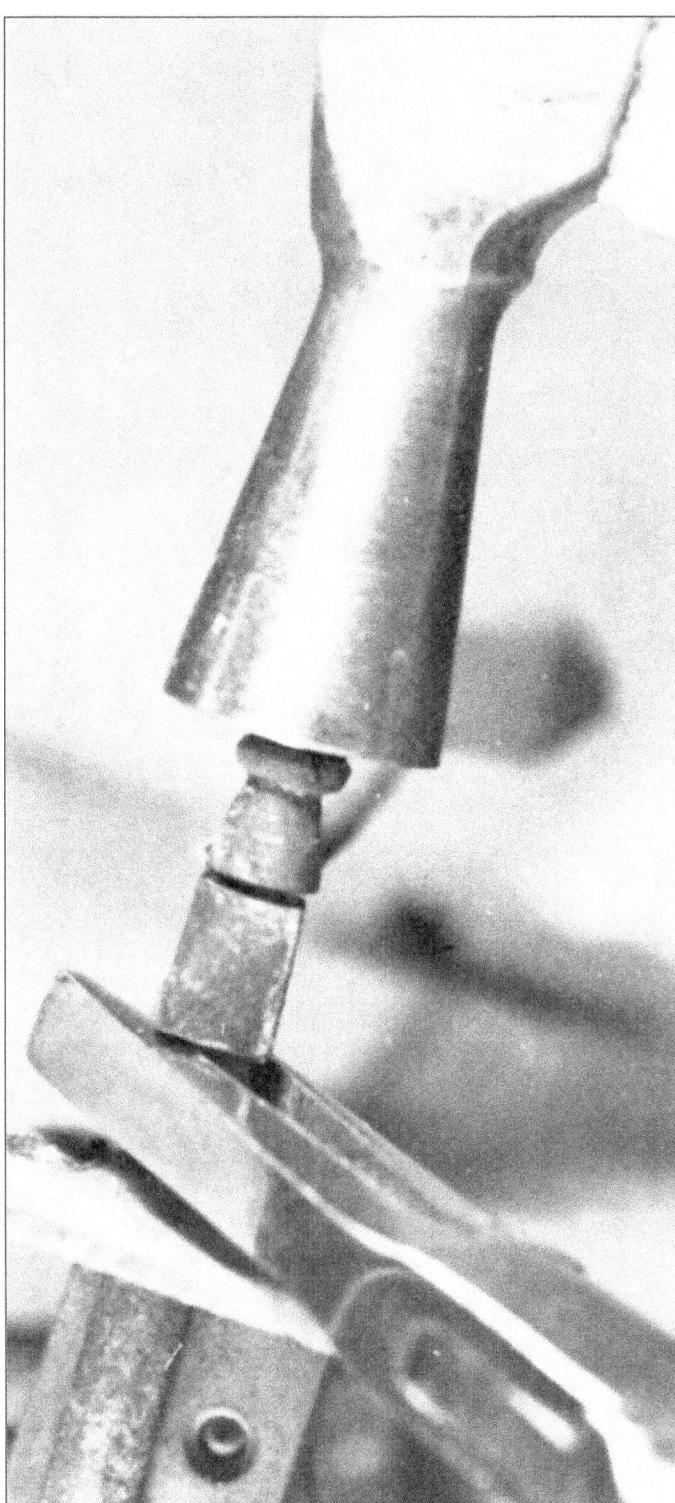

Figure 83. Freeing the hammer from the hammer arbor.

Figure 84. Independent half-hour strike in early nineteenth-century clock.

Figure 85. Another independent half-hour strike found on one-hand early eighteenth-century clocks.

Remove the alarm hammer if there is one. On earlier models there may also be an independent half-hour strike; if so, remove the half-hour hammer, its spring, and the release (Figures 84 and 85); replace the screws as necessary.

In disassembly always start with the strike train; see Figure 71 (page 45) for the parts of the strike train. First, remove the strike release with its jointed trip piece (Figure 86). It is a good idea to replace the strike release cock and its screw on the post.

Probably you will find the screws holding the mounting posts are marked with one to four dots of a center punch, and the corresponding punches are near the base of the mounting posts. Remove the screw at the top of the rear mounting post on the strike side, and with the clock face down, pull the top end of the mounting post gently but firmly to the rear of the clock. You will see that the top of the mounting bar has a slight projection that slides in a groove in the underside of the top plate (Figure 87). When the top end is free of the plate, the

Figure 86. Loosening the strike release cock to remove the strike release.

Figure 87. Underside of top plate showing score marks that help to fix the mounting bars in position.

lower end can be lifted free from the two holes in which projections on the legs fit. Then remove the detent (Figure 88), the fly, the stop wheel, the strike wheel, and the barrel. The latter is usually marked with an "S" on the end away from the click. If not, you should mark it so it won't be confused with the time train barrel. Cut the weight cord next to the barrel and remove the knot from inside the barrel. Finally, remove the front mounting post.

For the time train you again start by removing the rear mounting post. If it's an anchor escapement, remove the escape wheel, the third wheel, second wheel, and barrel; again note or mark the latter with an "M" for movement, and remove the cord. For the verge escapement, be sure to remove the escape wheel as soon as you remove the rear mounting post to avoid bending or breaking the pivots. To do this, remove the screw of the escape wheel cock on the top of the cage and remove the cock. Lift the escape wheel straight up until free of the lower support or potence and then take it out. Remove the verge, the contrate wheel, the second wheel, and barrel. Figure 89 shows a variation where the potence or lower pivot support of the escape wheel is mounted on the rear mounting post. In this particular movement the escape wheel must be removed

Figure 88. From bottom to top: barrel, strike wheel with ratchet, stop wheel, and detent. Strike release arbor at upper left and trip piece at center. The fly has been removed in this photo.

Figure 89. Variation in construction with potence fastened to rear mounting post spring side. Note date 1826 stamped at center post. The initials MJJ are also stamped on it.

Figure 90. Early model clock having escape wheel with teeth on top.

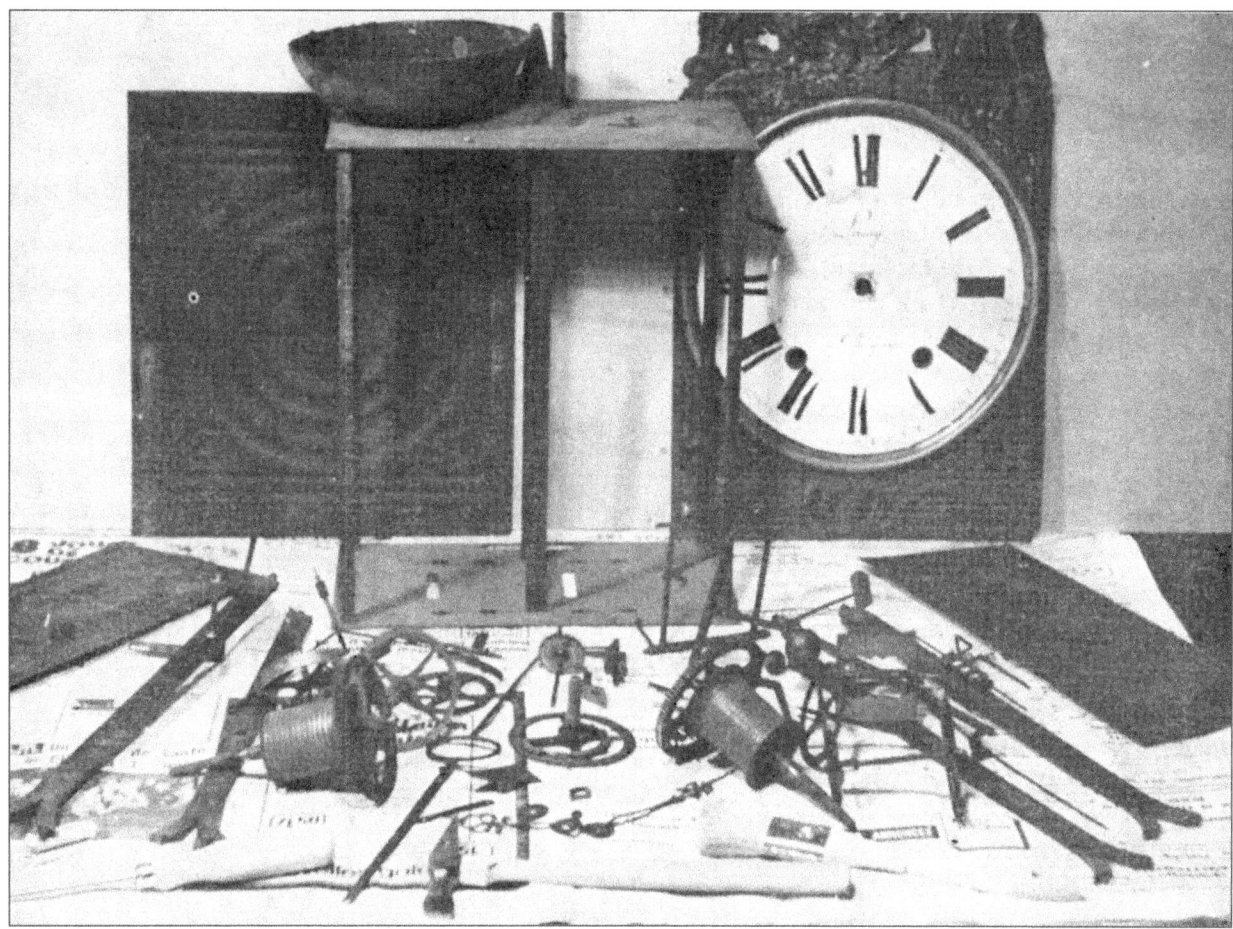

Figure 91. The clock completely disassembled ready to start cleaning.

before the rear mounting post is removed to avoid bending or breaking the pivots of the escape wheel arbor. Figure 90 shows a mid-eighteenth century movement with an inverted escape wheel (i.e., with teeth upward as in an English lantern clock). You may find other variations that require special handling to avoid damage as mentioned above. Remove the front mounting post, leaving the lower cock or potence of the escape wheel in place on it.

You now have the clock all in pieces and are ready to start the cleaning (Figure 91).

Cleaning

It is a good idea to start with the cage. If it is not rusted, all that may be needed is to wash it well in mineral spirits and peg out any of the pivot holes that are found in the posts or plates. You should check to see that the cage has not been distorted or bent (i.e., the posts should be perpendicular to the plates, both front to back and across). One clock I worked on had been dropped, apparently from a considerable height, and landed on one corner; the cage was considerably distorted.

If the cage is badly rusted, soak it in kerosene for a few days, and then use emery cloth or steel wool to clean off the rust. After rinsing in mineral spirits to get rid of the abrasives or steel wool shreds, the cage can be painted with a flat black enamel. The so-called wrought iron black is a good background for the bright steel parts and the brass wheels.

If the mounting posts and other bright steel parts have spots of heavy rust, they should be soaked in kerosene for a few days and then cleaned with an emery cloth. If the wheels or other brass parts have heavy corrosion (green stains), they should first be cleaned with steel wool or a fine emery cloth so that the cleaning fluid can work more effectively.

Clean all the parts except the cage in clock-cleaning fluid to remove traces of old oil and to brighten the brass. Follow the directions of the cleaning fluid maker concerning rinsing and drying. Although the wheels are usually not polished like the more refined French clocks, they do look better if you go over them with French chalk and a medium hard brush. If you like a really bright finish, use brass polish, tooth brush, and rags, but be sure to rinse in mineral spirits, and after drying, brush well with a clean brush and chalk to get rid of the abrasive and the chemical that gets in the tight places and shows up green in a few weeks or months. In the last stages you should hold the wheels with a clean rag to avoid fingerprints, which will act as a starting point for tarnish later.

Clean the pivot holes in the mounting posts with pegwood, paying particular attention to the oil sinks, which may have a heavy gob of hardened oil. The edges of the mounting posts and other steel parts were originally burnished bright in the

57

better quality clocks, whereas the flat sides were given a satin finish. It is satisfactory, however, to go over all surfaces with a medium emery buff and see that the last few strokes are parallel to the long dimension of the piece.

The dial surround can also be brightened up with the clock-cleaning solution, but be sure to rinse it well in clean water, shake the loose water off, and dry it with gentle heat to avoid rust on the black metal backing. Here again you can leave the dial surround with an overall matte finish. The repousse brass looks better, however, if you polish the highlights with brass polish, but again rinse, dry, and brush well to avoid the green stains. Do not use chalk on the dial surround because it tends to darken rather than brighten the metal.

Checking and Restoring before Assembly

Now that the parts are all clean yon can begin to check the parts and make necessary repairs. First check the barrels and barrel arbors; the winding squares are usually worn and may be deformed because a key that was too large has been used. Rather than file away a large amount of material to regain the square corners, it is usually possible to hammer them back into shape on an anvil since the arbors are quite soft. When the shape is almost right, a few touches with a file will dress it properly, and the size will not be unduly reduced. A new key should be selected so that there is a good fit over a reasonable bearing area. The ends of the arbors that show should be burnished to give a nice finish to the completed clock. After all, those two points and the minute hand arbor are the only parts of the movement that show in the finished job, so they deserve a little extra work.

Check the click on each barrel and make sure that it engages firmly in each tooth of the ratchet. Make sure the click screw is tight and the threads are not stripped. If so, tap the hole for a larger thread and fit a new screw.

Examine all the pivots for grooves and burnish them. Examine the pallets of the verge escapement to see if they show signs of wear. If the pallets have not been oiled, even after many years they will show little wear, but if some misguided mechanic has oiled them in the past, they may be badly grooved. If not too deep, the grooves can be stoned out with an oval oilstone slip or a fine emery buff, ending up with strokes parallel to the motion of the escape wheel. In either case, rinse off all traces of abrasive with mineral spirits. The pallets of an anchor escapement should also be checked and, if grooved, should also be corrected as with any other anchor escapement.

Figure 92. Lower potence with screw to adjust depth of pivots.

Reassembly and Checking the Time Train

In reassembling, always begin with the front mounting post of the time train. First, fit the bottom legs in place; then fit the projection at the top of the post into the groove as in Figure 87 (see page 53), push the top back into place, and fasten with the screw. Next, for clocks with the verge or crown wheel escapement, put the crown wheel in place, fasten the upper cock, and then check to see if the wheel turns freely and has end play. Check to make sure that the rounded end of the lower pivot rests on the potence or support bracket and that the shoulder does not touch the potence. On some clocks you will find an end screw that can be adjusted to adjust the depth of the pallets (Figure 92).

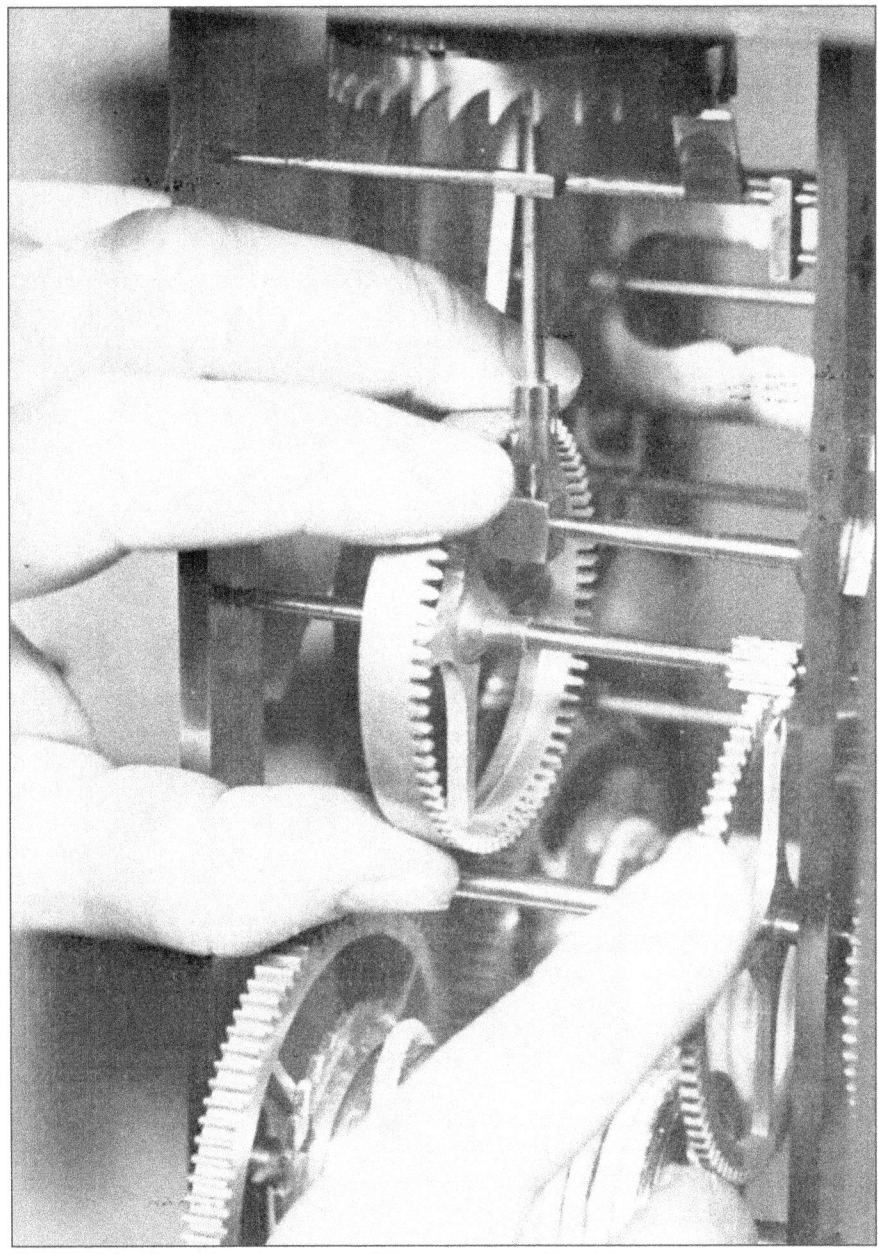

Figure 93. Checking the wear of the pivots and bushings.

This can be adjusted to lift the shoulder clear of the potence, but later when the pallets are being adjusted for locking and drop, make sure the shoulder does not rest on the potence. If it does, the potence will have to be bent as described below. If there isn't such a screw, the top surface of the potence will have to be filed to provide clearance. When this has been taken care of, add the verge, the contrate wheel, the second wheel, and the barrel and put the rear mounting post in place. Check the movement of the pivots in their holes to see if there is enough wear to interfere with the depths. The usual way is to hold the contrate wheel with one hand and move the second wheel with the other as shown in Figure 93.

Do this with the second wheel and the barrel as well. Because of the substantial pivots and the wide tolerances of the gearing, it is usually not necessary to replace a bushing. But if it is necessary, follow the usual procedures for locating the new hole before drilling out the old bushing. The new bushing is riveted in place and drilled to a size somewhat smaller than the pivot and then reamed to size with a cutting broach and finished with a smoothing broach. After such repairs, remove the verge and check to see that the train runs freely. In particular, on the verge escapement check the depthing of the contrate wheel and the crown wheel pinion. The contrate wheel must have end play or shake, but it should be minimal; and both the contrate wheel and the escape wheel should turn perfectly flat to preserve the depthing as the wheels turn. The pivots of the escape wheel arbor also must be straight; if bent, they will change the depthing of the contrate wheel and cause trouble.

When this is all in order, check the action of the escapement. Push the second wheel forward with one finger while operating the verge with the other hand. Make sure that the locking is sure and equal for both pallets. For the verge escapement it should be at least one millimeter or 1/25 of an inch (Figure 94). To increase the locking, lower the escape wheel by bending the potence (Figure 95). To decrease the locking, raise the escape wheel. On some very old Morbiers, you may find the verge above the escape wheel as in English lantern clocks (see Figure 90 on page 56). For such clocks you would, of course, lower the escape wheel. It is always safer to loosen the cock or even remove the escape wheel to avoid bending or breaking pivots when bending the potence. Usually only a very small adjustment is necessary.

Unequal locking can be caused by a displaced crown wheel or bent verge. The axes of the escape wheel and the verge should be perpendicular and the axis of the verge should be parallel to the plane of the tips of the escape wheel teeth. It is unusual to find irregularities here, but in case of abuse or damage you may have to put things right.

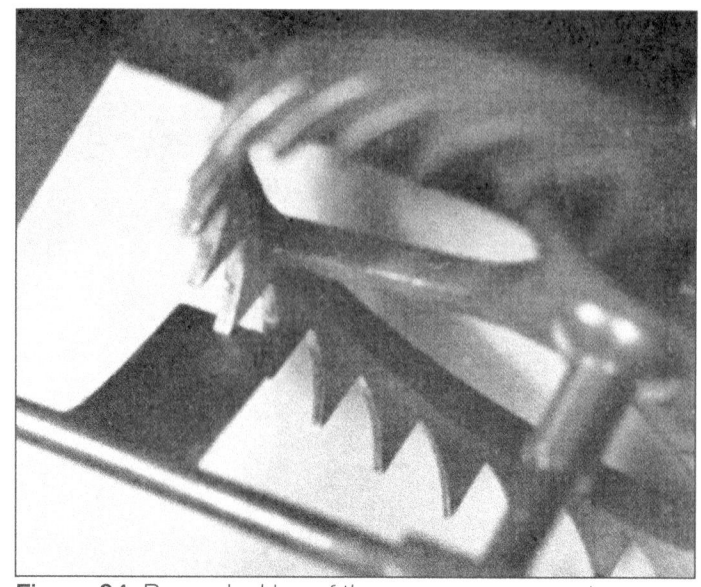

Figure 94. Proper locking of the verge escapement.

Next, check the drop, which should be about one millimeter (1/25 inch) and equal for both pallets and for all teeth of the escape wheel (Figure 96). To correct unequal drops on the pallets, bend the potence or lower bracket of the escape wheel to the right or left, again after loosening the upper cock or removing the escape wheel. If the drop is unequal on one or more teeth, look for an out-of-round or out-of-flat escape wheel or for bent or broken escape wheel teeth. Correcting these is more difficult and should be undertaken only if, in fact, the clock will not run satisfactorily. The verge or crown wheel escapement found in the Morbier clock is tolerant of irregularities that would stop an anchor escapement, so it is prudent to make only the minimum changes to make the clock run satisfactorily. If one or two of the teeth are shorter because of wear or damage, it is feasible to reduce the height of all teeth in the lathe and then restore the clearance by dressing the backs or curved sides of the teeth with a file. Do not touch the front or straight side of the tooth unless you have a dividing head with 31 divisions, in which case you can true up the wheel by machine. If the height of the teeth is reduced, you will have to restore the locking by lowering the escape wheel. This can be done by bending the lower potence or

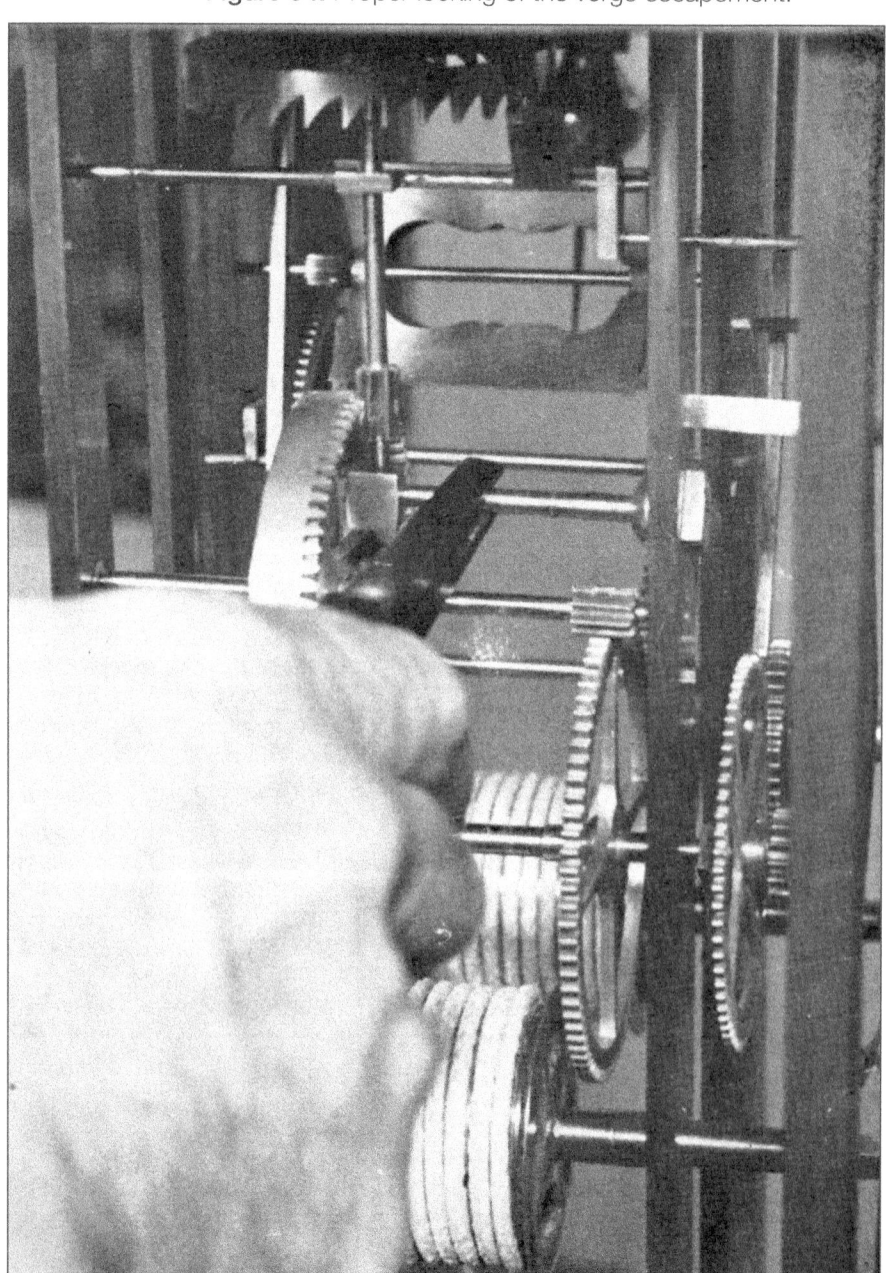

Figure 95, right. Adjusting the locking by bending the lower potence.

Figure 96. Proper amount of drop; this tooth has just escaped and the pallet on the other side is beginning recoil.

Motion Work

With the escapement and going train in order, continue by assembling the motion work. Put the minute wheel friction spring on the second wheel arbor, which has a slight taper, and make sure that it does not rub on the mounting post. If it does, reduce the size of the hole by peening the center of the spring and enlarge to size with a cutting broach, or else drill out and rivet in a new center that is drilled and broached to the proper size. When all is in order, oil this pivot before placing the spring in position for final assembly because it is inaccessible later. Place the intermediate wheel on the arbor and replace the pin, making sure that the ends of the pins do not extend beyond the base of the hour pinion leaves (Figure 97). Check the friction of the drive to make sure it is sufficient to drive the hands, to lift the strike detent, and to operate the independent or passing half-hour strike, if there is one. Put the cannon wheel in place and fasten the cock. Check the depthing of the intermediate wheel in the cannon wheel.

Figure 97. Proper length of pin securing intermediate wheel of motion work.

bracket as mentioned before, but be careful not to change the equality of the locking on the two pallets.

A broken tooth can be replaced by filing an appropriate notch in the rim of the escape wheel and soldering or riveting in a piece of brass, which is then shaped to match the other tooth. There is usually plenty of material to work with in the rim of the escape wheel, but each situation should be carefully studied before any cutting is done.

In most cases you will find that very little has to be done to the crown wheel or verge escapement to put it in running order. The small angle of the pallets and the length and flexibility of the pendulum cause most of the weaknesses of this type of escapement to disappear. Nevertheless, if you have the unlucky tenth, the foregoing should help in identifying the malfunction and correcting it.

The anchor escapements found in Morbiers made during the late nineteenth century and up until World War I are simple and rugged and easily repaired. If the pallets are worn, the pits should be stoned out or nearly so and the locking restored by moving the eccentric bushing, which is usually found in the front mounting bar. Excessive drop is corrected by bending in the pallets, but again usually such adjustments are not needed unless the clock has been damaged or abused.

Assembling and Checking the Strike Train

As with the time train, we start with the front mounting post. Make sure that the rack is free to slide up and down but without too much play in the guides. Place the barrel, the strike wheel, the stop wheel, and the fly in place, and check the wear of the pivots and holes. If all is in order, add the detent, the strike hammer arbor, the strike hammer spring and then adjust the relation of the strike wheel to the stop wheel as follows: When the stop pin is against the detent, the hammer should not be lifted (i.e., there should be a slight clearance between the tooth of the strike ratchet and the projection of the hammer arbor). Push on the strike wheel in the direction of motion to check this, and then release the detent. The stop wheel should move from 1/8 to 1/4 of a turn before the hammer arbor starts to move. If this does not occur, ease the rear mounting bar back at the top until you can adjust the strike wheel and the stop wheel pinion, moving it one leaf forward or back as necessary. Push the rear mounting bar back into position, fitting the other pivots in their holes and try again. Make a further readjustment if necessary and when all is in order, fasten the rear mounting bar into position.

Examine the relationship of the stop pin and the detent. With the rack at the top of its travel and the gathering pawl in the last and deepest tooth or notch, the stop pin should rest on the detent about its own diameter from the corner (Figure 98). If less, it might slip, and if more, it may not always release. Adjust by bending the arm of the detent that engages the rack.

Now check the function of the rack. The extended leaf of the stop wheel pinion should engage each tooth of the rack sufficiently so that it lifts the rack slightly more than the height of one tooth to ensure that the gathering pawl on the other side properly engages the next tooth. If the rack is not lifted sufficiently, the guide wires should be bent so that the rack engages the extended pinion leaf a little more deeply, which will cause it to be lifted a little higher. In bending the guide wires make sure that the depth is the same when the rack is at the lowest and the highest positions. Make sure that the gathering pawl is free to move to the bottom of the last tooth or notch of the rack, which brings the detent into position to arrest the stop pin.

In clocks that depend on counterweights to operate the detent and strike release, it is important to have the clock level when checking the operation of these various parts. If you study the action of the strike mechanism, you will see that the counterweights work against each other, and any displacement from the level may interfere with a proper check of the functioning.

Put the strike release in place and fasten the cock with its screw. Check the functioning of the strike release as follows: When the strike release forked arm is ready to drop in the notch of the strike release cam with the strike train arrested by the detent and stop pin, there should be a clearance of one millimeter (1/25 inch) between the trip piece and the detent

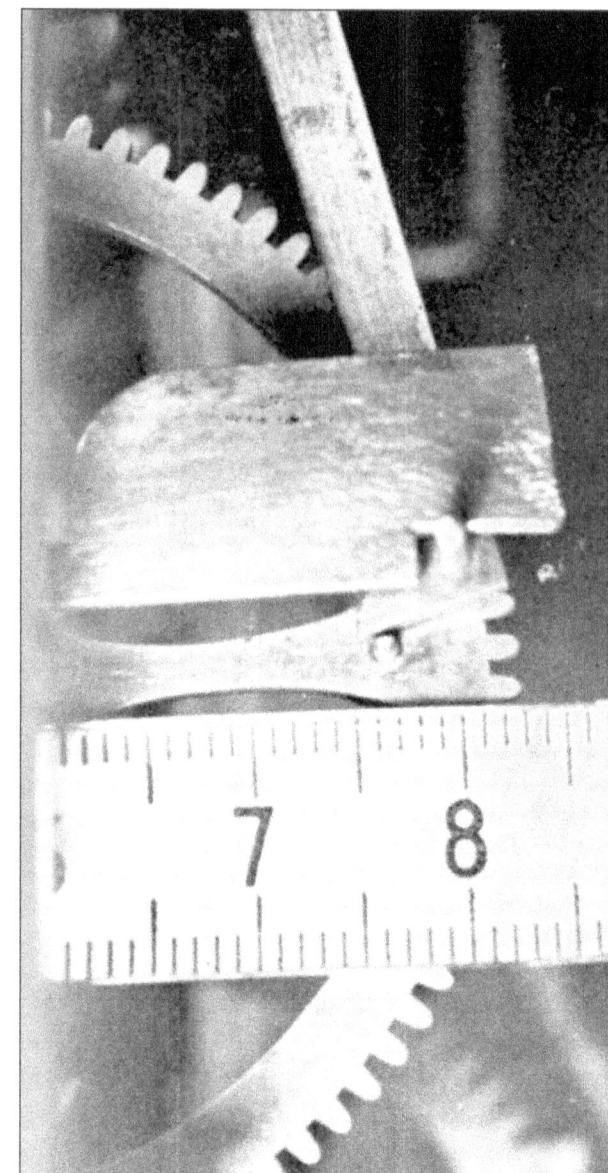

Figure 98. Proper relation of stop pin and detent when strike train is arrested and clearance of 1 millimeter between trip piece and pin in detent just before release of repeat hour strike.

(Figure 99). If it is more or less, bend the strike release arm in the needed direction, being careful not to damage the cam or other parts of the mechanism. Figures 98 and 99 are printed about twice actual size.

When this is correct, cause the hour to strike by moving the cannon slowly and stop before the repeat strike occurs. Again check the clearance—it should be about the same (Figure 98). If not, the second branch of the forked arm should be adjusted. The same clearance should be maintained just before the half-hour strike.

Trip the strike several times to make sure that the stop pin is released and that the rack falls all the way to the bottom on the hour and the repeat. If it does not function properly, examine the strike release cam. It may be deformed or even broken, probably because someone turned the hands backward.

obvious that the mechanism was functioning at one time, and your job is to make the minimum changes to get it working again. In case of accidental damage, of course, you will have to try to imagine how the parts were originally or examine another clock that is functioning properly. If there is evidence that another mechanic has changed things to improve the action, you really have a problem, but that is quite unlikely.

In the earlier Morbiers the strike action is dependent on the relative strength of two springs rather than on counterweights (Figure 100). The strike release lever spring is considerably stronger than the detent spring so that when the strike release lever drops off the cam at the hour and the repeat, the trip piece moves with sufficient force to push the detent back against its spring and release the stop wheel of the train. In disassembly, cleaning, and reassembly, one or both of these springs may be distorted so that the relative strength is not proper. In such cases the clock may not strike at all or it may run away. Close observation and some reflection will indicate the corrections to be made.

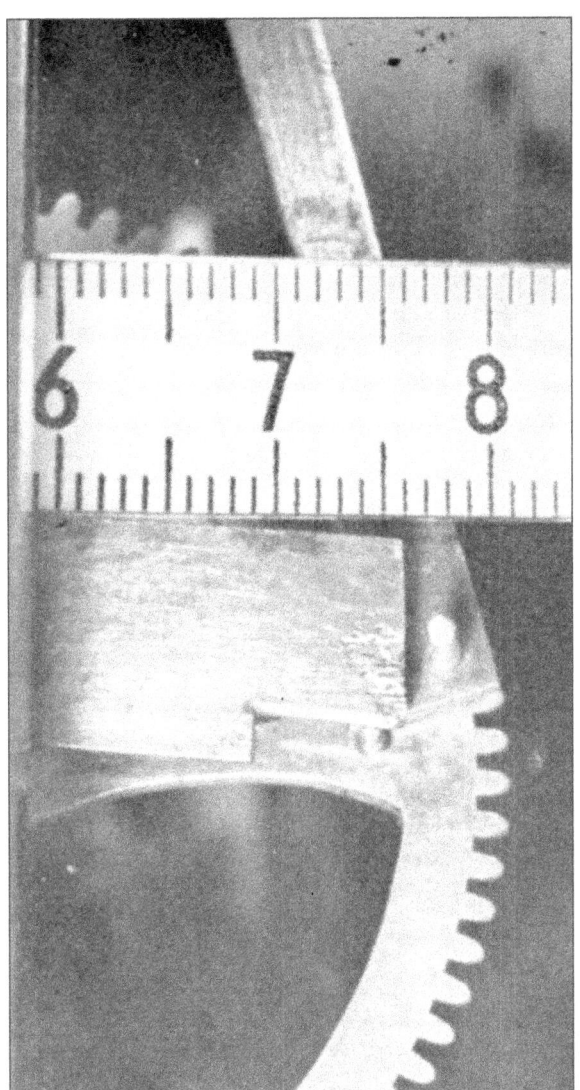

Figure 99. Clearance of millimeter (1/25 inch) between trip piece and pin or projecting lug on detent just before release for the first hour.

Make sure that at the half hour the rack stays firmly on the gathering pawl of the detent and that the stop pin is still able to be released.

The long pin near the hub of the stop wheel lifts the trip piece, allowing the detent to move into each notch and finally into the deep notch of the rack and arrest the train. Make sure that this pin is not bent or broken and that the trip piece is lifted well before the rack begins to lift. In most clocks, the lifting pawl is an extension of one pinion leaf, and this relation cannot be changed unless the stop wheel is loose on the arbor. On a few clocks, however, the lifting pawl is separate from the pinion, and it may get out of position.

If you have problems, study the mechanism and refrain from filing any parts or making changes in the basic geometry. You may also want to refer back to the earlier sections on striking trains where additional explanations and descriptions are given. It is

Figure 100. Earlier model Morbier with springs rather than counterweights.

Final Assembly

Now that the time and strike trains are in good operating condition, we are ready for the final assembly. It is a good idea to fit new weight cords because the old ones are probably not dependable, and a seven- or eight-pound weight hitting the floor makes quite a hole.

The clocks originally had a hard twisted cord that was lint free. This cord was still obtainable in France, but in the United States it is probably better to use a nylon cord of about the same diameter. Thread the cord through the hole in the barrel from the outside, pull out through one of the holes in the end of the barrel, and tie a good sized knot. The loose end should be cut off quite short to avoid getting it caught in the mechanism. Pull the knot back inside and cut off the cord about seven feet long. Attach the hook securely with a double knot. If the hooks are missing, form "S" hooks about 1-1/4 inch overall out of some heavy wire (an old coat hanger does well), being sure to close one loop tight for the cord. It is a good idea to place a large washer with a small hole on the cord above the hook. This prevents the hook from passing through the slot in the bottom plate of the cage. When this happens, it often gets caught, and it is a frustrating task to get it back down through the slot again. You occasionally find old coins that had lost their value drilled and used for this purpose.

Sometimes you find that one weight has a Roman numeral VII and the other VIII. This usually is the weight in pounds and the heavier or eight-pound weight is for the strike train.

Under Dial Work

At this point it is convenient to set the clock on a clock horse or some other support at a suitable height with free access on all sides and hang the weights on the hooks.

Turn the cannon wheel so that it is ready to release the strike. Place the hour hand on the hour wheel pipe, so that it points between the twelve (the lowest step) and the one (the highest step) of the snail. Then place the hour wheel on the cannon arbor with the hour hand pointing toward twelve. With the strike weight in place, release the strike by turning the intermediate wheel slowly counterclockwise. The rack and its control rod should climb up freely without rubbing against the snail or the hour wheel. Make sure the number of blows corresponds to the hour indicated at the first strike; then move the cannon arbor to release the second strike and check again. Try all the hours and especially 11 o'clock, where the step on the snail is the smallest. If it doesn't strike right, shift the hour wheel one tooth ahead or behind, and for fine adjustment bend the rod slightly to the right or left. Don't file or hammer the end of the control rod. If the strike is off by one blow for all hours, bend the rod right next to the rack until the number of notches on the rack when it falls corresponds to the hour.

If the clock has a string suspension, replace the old string with heavy carpet and button thread or braided fishing line. Avoid heavy bulky cord. Hang the pendulum on the pendulum rod and adjust the length of the string so that the pendulum rod doesn't touch the interior of the steeple or any other part of the movement and the stirrup clears the hour hand pipe. Check the suspension spring on clocks that are so equipped and replace it if it is kinked or broken. Check the operation of the escapement. With the clock level, the suspension rod should be the same distance from the center line on both sides when the drop occurs. If it isn't, bend the verge rod as required. At this stage a clock horse or other solid level support at a convenient working height is especially helpful.

Oil the front or dial side of the clock with good clock oil; you should already have oiled the pivot of the minute wheel, which is inaccessible behind the friction spring. Oil all the pivots in the back of the clock, the pivots of the hammer, and the barrel ratchets. Don't oil the strike release arm.

Do not put oil on the escape wheel teeth or the pallets of a crown wheel escapement. It only causes wear and trouble, as explained earlier. Do not oil the guide wires of the rack; they should be clean and dry and slide freely.

Add the calendar idler wheel if there is one and the calendar star wheel, adjusting the depth of the pin in the star wheel and the jumper spring as necessary. Check that the star wheel advances at about the 12 o'clock position, and make necessary adjustments of the relation of the idler wheel to the drive wheel on the hour hand pipe. The alarm snail and its release and the alarm weight cord should be put on at this time for clocks with alarms. Also, the independent half-hour strike hammer, release, and spring should be put in place (see Figures 84 and 85 on page 52). Check to see if it releases exactly on the half hour by putting the minute hand temporarily on its arbor. Make any necessary adjustments but avoid drastic measures.

If you have checked out all the points mentioned above, there should be no reason why the clock should not run and strike properly. Nevertheless, you may want to set the clock running for a few hours or days to make sure before putting on the face, the back, and the side doors. It is much easier to make the final adjustments without these being in the way; besides, you have the chance to really get acquainted with this wonderful mechanism.

When you are sure all is in order, put on the dial and fasten with the two screws at the upper corners. Put on the alarm ring, if there is one, which clips onto the alarm snail; it should only fit one way, but there is a possibility of having it six hours off. Put on the calendar hand if there is one. When it is properly fixed, put on the hour hand and fasten with the square. If it is loose, you may have to hammer it a bit or bend it to grip the hour wheel cannon and fix the hour hand firmly.

Place the minute hand and turn it to ascertain when the hour strike occurs and then fix the minute hand in the 12 o'clock position with the large washer under the nut. Check that the hands do not interfere with each other and keep the minute hand reasonably close to the dial.

Figure 101. Alarm hammer in neutral position to avoid rattling noise when clock is striking hours.

Put on the bell hammer and the bell; remember the leather washers above and below the bell. Adjust the hammer so that it strikes the bell right at the edge, and check that it doesn't rest against the bell after striking. If there is an alarm, also check that the alarm hammer hits both ends evenly when ringing and is retained in the neutral position when not striking (Figure 101); otherwise, it may rattle against the bell when the hours are being struck. Put the back on and replace the side doors by putting the upper pivot in its hole, springing the plate slightly to reduce its height as shown in Figure 73 (see page 47), and then slipping the lower pivot in its hole. The latch may have to be adjusted so that it keeps the door firmly closed and also holds itself by friction.

The clock is now ready to put in place on a wall bracket or in the case, if you have one. The usual precautions should be taken to level and brace the case against lateral movement and then level the clock in the case, using thin wooden wedges or hard cardboard shims as necessary. With the light pine cases, it is particularly important to fasten them to the wall because they are quite shallow from front to back and quite unstable when the weights are at the top.

NOTES

The term "verge escapement" is used in this article for brevity and is meant to be equivalent to the term "crown wheel escapement."

1. In the list of former clock and watchmakers in Britten there is a record of Pierre Claude Mayet as a maker of three public clocks within a radius of about 30 miles of Morbier from 1687 to 1729. His son, Pierre Francois, made a clock for Bourg-en-Bresse, a little farther away in 1733. No mention is made of domestic clocks by these makers.

One is apt to think that without newspapers, radio, or even a postal service, communication between Paris and a remote area such as the Jura would be slow or even impossible. For example, the news of Huygen's successful application of the pendulum to clocks took 25 years to reach Morbier. But, curiously enough, news of the work of the Mayet brothers and others in the Jura soon reached Paris. In the "Traite de l'Horlogerie" published in 1741, Antoine Thiout shows a pivoted pallet escapement for tower clocks, which he says "was invented by the Maillets of Morbier and Bellefontaine in the Franche-Comte." This is in a section of the book where he also shows escapements of well-known clockmakers such as Graham, du Tertre, and Amant, inventor of the pinwheel escapement. In this same book Thiout also mentions that he has seen an equation clock and a new celestial globe made by Jean Baptiste Catin, of Fort du Plane, a hamlet near Foncine-le-Bas. One wonders how word of what was going on in the Jura reached Paris in those times, to be noted by Thiout in his review of the state of the art of clock and watchmaking in the mid-eighteenth century.

2. The French word for the metal piece above or in some cases surrounding the dial is *fronton* and is borrowed from architectural terms where it means pediment or gable over an entrance or doorway. It is related to the French word *front,* or

forehead. In this article, it is translated as "front" and should be taken to mean the cast bronze or embossed brass piece above or around the dial, and not the dial itself.

3. In deCarle's book *Practical Clock Repairing* (p. 212 of the 1951 edition), he mentions Dr. Rawlings' article in the *Horological Journal* of 1950. The proportions mentioned by Rawlings are quite extreme, and while theoretically efficient, the very small engagement of the pallets in the escape wheel (0.004 inch) would seem to be impractical in a clock for everyday use. Saunier discusses the design of a clock escapement where the angle between the pallets is only 14 degrees, but as far as I have been able to determine, escapements of such proportions were not made in the Jura or elsewhere.

4. It is curious that Ward Goodrich in his otherwise very complete book, *The Modern Clock*, seems to have been completely unaware of the Morbier. Written originally in 1905 when these clocks had just passed their peak of production, he notes in his introduction that French clocks are of two classes: carriage clocks and pendules, by which he apparently meant mantel clocks. His very complete treatment of pinwheel escapements shows he was aware of other French developments. The fact that he does not mention the verge escapement at all probably indicates he did not consider it should be included in a book dealing with "the modern clock."

BIBLIOGRAPHY

Note: Very little has been written in any language about the Morbier clock. Nevertheless, the following references may be of interest. (Editor's note: This listing includes books available through the NAWCC Library and Research Center that were not available when Lawrence Seymour's articles were originally published in the NAWCC BULLETIN.)

Dutch
Bollen, Ton. *Comtoiseklokken*. Bussum, Holland: Unieboek, 1974.

English Language
Britten, Baille, Clutton, and Ilbert, eds. *Old Clocks and Watches and Their Makers*, 7th ed. New York: Bonanaza Books, 1956: pp. 228-230.

Nemrava, Steve Z. *The Morbier: 1680-1900*. Portland, OR: Nemrava, 1975.

Maitzner, Francis, and Jean Moreau. *Comtoise Clocks: The Morbier, the Morez*, 5th ed., first English ed. Translated by Lawrence Alan Seymour. Dombasle: Stampa P. Forignon, 1991.

Royer-Collard, F. B. Letter in *NAWCC BULLETIN*, No. 144 (February 1970): pp. 193-194.

Saunier, Claudius. *Treatise on Modern Horology*. Trans. by Tripplin and Rigg. London: W. & G. Foyle Ltd., 1952: pp. 56, 61, 63-73, 541-543, 569-573.

Tardy. *The French Clocks. Part Three: From the Louis-Philippe Style to the Modern Clock and the French Provinces*, 5th ed. Paris: Tardy, 1981-1985.

French Language
Beausoleil, Oscar. *Editions Techniques*. Paris: Horlogerie Reparations, 1957.

Bienne, Switzerland, material originally appeared in *Journal Suiss d'Horlogerie* (1932-1935).

Caudine, Alain. *La Grande horloge: La Comtoise au xix siecle*. Paris: Les Editions de L'Amateur, 1992.

Gagnant, L. *La Pendule de Morez*. Besançon & Morez, France: Administration de L'Union Professionelle, 1912.

Horloges de parquet horloges comtoises: collections privees de Franche-Comte. Besancon: ANCAHA, 1975. Small exhibit catalog; exhibit held September 1975.

Jaquet, Eugene and Dante Gibertini. *La Reparation des Pendules*, 1958.

Maitzner, Francis, and Jean Moreau. *La Comtoise, la Morbier, La Morez: son historie, sa technique, ses particularites, ses complications, sa reparation*. France: Maitzner and Moreau, 1976.

Olivier, Jean-Marc. *Des clous, des horloges et des lunettes: les campagnards moréziens en industrie (1780-1914)*. Paris: Éditions du CTHS, 2004.

Rosset, Emile. "LaComtoise (Morbier)." *Bulletin of the Association Nationale des collectionneurs et amateurs d'Horlogerie Ancienne*, No. 2 (April 1969).

German
Bergmann, Siegfried. *Comtoise-uhren*. Stolberg, Germany: La Pendule, 2005.

Deckert, Bernd. *Die Geschichte der Comtoise Uhren*. Germany: Comtoise Uhren Museum, 2008.

Schmitt, Gustav. *Die Comtoiser uhr*. Villingen, Germany: Verlag Müller, 1979.

To Experience Adventures in TIME...
Join the NAWCC

It All Starts with Membership

The National Association of Watch and Clock Collectors, Inc. (NAWCC) is an international nonprofit association serving more than 17,000 members and 150 chapters and dedicated to preserving and stimulating interest in horology, the art and science of time. Our members are enthusiasts, students, educators, casual collectors, businesses, and professionals, who love learning about the clocks and watches they preserve, study, and collect. Members share their interests with other members and establish friendships around the world.

Membership Advantages

- Stay informed with the bimonthly *Watch & Clock Bulletin*, an educational journal, and the *Mart & Highlights*, a buy/sell/news publication.
- Go online for research tools and videos: NAWCC.org features all *Watch & Clock Bulletin* content back to 1943, NAWCC books and instructional videos, and much more for members.

- Buy, sell, and learn at regional buying and selling venues, and attend programs on all aspects of horology.
- Keep in touch with our bimonthly electronic newsletter—*eHappenings*
- Meet terrific people at local and special interest chapters
- Visit for free the National Watch & Clock Museum in Columbia, PA.
- Use your membership for free or discounted admission to over 250 museums and science centers.

Become a member today and begin your exploration of the fascinating world of horology.

Apply online at www.nawcc.org

Become a member today!
Mail this application,
apply online at www.nawcc.org,
or call 1-877-255-1849 or 1-717-684-8261.

*Required fields

*Print Name

Company Name (optional)

*Street

*City

*State/Province/Country   *Zip/Postal Code

( )   ( )
Ph.: Home   Work

( )   ( )
Cell   Fax

Email

☐ I agree to abide by the NAWCC Member Code of Ethical Conduct (see nawcc.org to review).

*Are you a former member of NAWCC? ☐ Yes ☐ No

If "yes," your membership no.

/   /
Date of Birth Confidential for verification purposes. Required for Youth Membership.

Occupation

How did you learn about the NAWCC?
Interest: ☐ Clocks ☐ Wristwatches ☐ Pocket Watches ☐ Museum
From:

If this is a gift membership, print your name above and a gift card will be included with the membership card mailing.

Send this application with payment to:
NAWCC, Inc., 514 Poplar Street, Columbia, PA 17512-2130
Annual dues:
☐ **Individual $82** (mailed pubs.) ☐ **Individual $72** (electronic publications)
☐ **Business $150** (mailed pubs.) ☐ **Assoc./Youth $20** (electronic pubs.)
                                        (Spouse) / (Under 18)
                                    ☐ **Student $35** (electronic pubs.)
                                        Proof of enrollment required for student membership. Please call for information.

Payment:
☐ **Check enclosed (U.S. bank only)** ☐ **Intl. Money Order**
☐ **Visa** ☐ **MasterCard** ☐ **Discover** ☐ **American Express**

Credit Card No.

/
Exp. Date   Security Code

Cardholder's Name   Amt. to be charged

Signature